No Tears in Heaven

C. H. Spurgeon

CHRISTIAN
HERITAGE

Charles Haddon Spurgeon is considered the great Victorian preacher. He left a legacy for modern times that made him known as the 'Prince of Preachers'.

Look out for *Living by Revealed Truth* by Tom Nettles (ISBN 978-1-78191-122-8). He has spent more than fifteen years working on this magisterial biography of Charles Haddon Spurgeon which covers his life and ministry, and also provides an in-depth survey of his theology.

Copyright © Christian Focus Publications 2014

paperback ISBN 978-1-78191-404-5
epub ISBN 978-1-78191-446-5
Mobi ISBN 978-1-78191-449-6

Published in 2014
by
Christian Focus Publications, Ltd.
Geanies House, Fearn, Ross-shire,
IV20 1TW, Scotland, United Kingdom.
www.christianfocus.com

Cover design by Daniel van Straaten

Printed by
Bell and Bain, Glasgow

MIX
Paper from
responsible sources
FSC® C007785

CONTENTS

1

A Prepared Place
for a Prepared People[1]

I go to prepare a place for you.
John 14:2

*Giving thanks unto the Father, which hath made us meet to
be partakers of the inheritance of the saints in light.*
Colossians 1:12

My real text is not in the Bible; it is one of those
Christian proverbs which are not inspired in
words, but the spirit of which is inspired, 'Heaven is
a prepared place for a prepared people.' You have often heard
that sentence; it is familiar in your mouths as household
words, and well it may be. Yet I shall have two texts from
the Scriptures; the first will be our Saviour's words to his

---

1. Sermon preached on Sunday evening, 25 May 1879, at the Metropolitan
    Tabernacle, Newington, London.

disciples, 'I go to prepare a place for you,' from which we learn that 'Heaven is a prepared place'; and the second will be Paul's words to the Colossians, 'Giving thanks unto the Father, which hath made us meet to be partakers of the inheritance of the saints in light,' from which we learn that there is a prepared people, a people made meet to be partakers of the inheritance which Christ has gone to prepare for them.

I am not going to have any further preface, but I will begin at once to speak upon the *Preparation of Heaven*: 'I go to prepare a place for you.'

It is many months since I began to turn this sentence over; I think I might truly say that, for several years, I have thought of it, and thought of it again, and thought of it yet again, that our Lord Jesus Christ, before returning to heaven, should say to his disciples, 'I go to prepare a place for you.' Is there any difficulty about this passage? Yes, it is very difficult to explain; indeed, I do not think that we really can know here all that Christ meant when he uttered these words.

A father said to his children, when the summer sun had waxed hot, 'I shall go to the seaside today, to prepare a place for you.' His little child asked, 'What does father mean when he says that he will prepare a place for us?' And his mother answered, 'My child, I cannot tell you all that your father means, but you will see when you get there; and now, it must be enough for you that, although you do not know what father will have to do at the seaside in preparing a place for you, he knows what he is going to do.' And, dear friends, there is this consolation for us that, even if we can hardly guess what it is that Christ can find to do to prepare heaven for us, he knows what is wanted, and he knows how to do it; and that is infinitely better than our knowing, because, even if we knew what was needed, we could not do it. But, with Christ, to know and to do are two things that run parallel.

He knows that there are certain preparations to be made, he knows what those preparations must be and he is equal to the task of making them; he has not gone upon an errand which he, cannot fulfil; and when we get to heaven, we shall know – perhaps it may take us a long while to find it all out – but we shall know and discover throughout eternity what he meant when he said, '*I* go to prepare a place for you.'

I do not profess to be able to explain our Lord's words, but I am going simply to make a few remarks upon them; and, first, I ask you to notice that *heaven is already prepared for Christ's people.* Christ has told us that, when he comes in his glory, he will say to those on his right hand: 'Come, ye blessed of my Father, inherit the kingdom prepared for you from the foundation of the world.' So, there is an inheritance which the Father has already prepared for the people whom he gave to his Son, and this inheritance is reserved for them. But if it was prepared from the foundation of the world, how can it be said to be prepared by Christ? The explanation probably is, that it was prepared in the eternal purpose of the Father – prepared by wise forethought – arranged for – predestinated – prepared in that sense – it was provided in the eternal arrangements of Jehovah that there should be a suitable place for his people to dwell in for ever. He made the pavilion of the sun, and he gave the stars their appointed positions; would he forget to prepare a place for his people? He gave to angels their places, and even to fallen spirits he has appointed a prison-house; so he would not forget, when he was arranging the entire universe, that a place would be needed for the twice-born, the heirs of grace, the members of the mystical body of Christ Jesus, his brethren who were to be made like unto him. Therefore, in purpose, and plan, and decree, long ere God had laid the foundations of this poor world, and the morning stars had sung together over creation's six days' work accomplished, he had prepared a place for his people; it was not actually prepared, but it was in the purpose and plan of the eternal mind, and therefore might be regarded as already done.

Our Lord Jesus Christ has gone to heaven, he says, that he may prepare a place for his servants, and we may be helped to form some idea of what he means by this expression if we just think a little about it. And, first, I am sure *that must be a very great and glorious place which needs Christ to prepare it*. If we do not know all that he means, we can get at least this much out of his declaration. He spake this world into being. It was not; but he said, 'Be,' and it was at once made. Then he spake it into order, into light, into life, into beauty. He had but to speak, and what he willed was done. But now that he is preparing a place for his people, he has gone to heaven on purpose to do it. He used to stand still here on earth, and work miracles; but this was a miracle that he could not perform while he was here. He had to go back to his home above in order to prepare a place for his people. What sort of place, then, must it be that needs Christ himself to prepare it? He might have said, 'Angels, garnish a mansion for my beloved.' He might have spoken to the firstborn sons of light, and said, 'Pile a temple of jewels for my chosen.' But, no, he leaves not the work to them; but he says, 'I go to prepare a place for you.'

Brethren, he *will do it well, for he knows all about us*. He knows what will give us the most happiness – and what will best develop all our spiritual faculties for ever. He loves us, too, so well that, as the preparing is left to him, I know that he will prepare us nothing second-rate, nothing that could possibly be excelled. We shall have the best of the best, and much of it; we shall have all that even his great heart can give us. Nothing will be stinted; for, as he is preparing it, it will be a right royal and divine preparation. If, when the prodigal came back to his father, there was the preparation of the fatted calf, and the music and dancing, and the gold ring and the best robe, what will be the preparation when we do not come home as prodigals, but as the bride prepared for her husband, or as the beloved children, without spot, or wrinkle, or any such thing, coming home to the Father who shall see his own image in us, and rejoice over us with singing? It is a grand place that Christ prepares, for never was there another such a lordly host as he is. It is a mansion of delights, I deem, that he prepares, for never was there another architect with thought so magnificent as his, and never were other hands so skilled at quarrying living stones, and putting them one upon another, as his hands have ever been. This thought ought to cheer us much; it must be something very wonderful that Christ prepares as a fit place for his people.

And methinks I may add to this, that *it must be something very sweet when it is prepared*. If you go to a friend's house, and just fall in with the ordinary proceedings of the family, you are very comfortable, and you are glad not to disarrange anything; but if, when you arrive, you see that everything has been done on an extra scale to prepare for your coming, you feel still more grateful. It has often happened to an honoured guest that he could not help observing that he was not being treated as his friends lived every day of the week, and all the year round. That guest-chamber had evidently been newly furnished, and everything that was possible had been thought of to do him honour. If you were treated thus as a guest, there was pleasure for you in the fact that so much had been prepared for you. Did your husband ever take you to a new house, and point out to you how he had purchased everything that he thought would please you? Had that little room been furnished specially for you, and did he anticipate your tastes, provide this little thing and that that he knew you would like? Well, it was not merely that you enjoyed the things themselves, but they all seemed to you so much sweeter because they had been prepared for you by your beloved. And when you get to heaven, you will be astonished to see this and that and the other joy that was prepared for you because Christ thought of you and provided just what you would most appreciate. You will be no stranger there, beloved: you will say, 'There has been here a hand that helped me, when I was in distress; there has been here, I know, an eye that saw me when I was wandering far from God; there has been, in this place, a heart that cared for me – that self-same heart that loved me, and that bled for me down below upon the cross. It is my Saviour who has prepared this place for me.'

I do not know whether I can convey to you all my thoughts upon this theme, but it does seem to me so pleasant to think that we are going to a place where we shall not be the first travellers through the country; but where *a Pioneer has gone before* us – the best of pioneers, who went before us with this one object in his mind, that he might get all ready and prepare the place for us. Methinks, brethren, that those who will be there before us will say, when we arrive there, 'We are glad you have come, for everything has been prepared for you.' It would be an eternal sorrow in heaven if the saints should miss their way, and perish, as some croakingly tell us; for, then, what about the preparations for their reception? They would all have been made in vain – harps prepared, which no fingers would ever play, and crowns which no heads would ever wear. I do not believe it; I have never dreamed that such a thing could happen. I feel certain that he, who prepared the place for the people, will prepare the people for the place; and that, if he gets all ready for them, he means to bring them home that they may enjoy the things which he hath laid up for them that love him.

I know that I am not explaining the preparation of heaven, yet I hope I am draining some comfortable thoughts out of the subject. If Christ is preparing heaven, then it will be what our Scotch friends call 'a bonnie place'; and if it be prepared for us, when we get there it will exactly fit us, it will be the very heaven we wanted – a better heaven than we ever dreamed of, a better heaven than we ever pictured even when our imagination took its loftiest flights – the heaven of God, and yet a heaven exactly suited to such happy creatures as we then shall be.

Now, however, let us try to come a little closer to the subject, and attempt to explain our Lord's words. Jesus Christ has gone to prepare a place for his people; does not this refer, if we keep it to its strict meaning, to *the ultimate place of God's people?* You see, Christ mentions a place, not a state; and he speaks of going to it, and coming back from it: 'I go to prepare a place for you. And if I go and prepare a place for you, I will come again, and receive you unto myself.' Christ is speaking of himself in his full manhood, without any figurative meaning to his words. He meant that he was going, with all his human nature on him, away from this world; and that he was going to prepare a place for us, intending to come again, with all that glorified human nature about him, to receive us unto himself.

This does not mean his spiritual coming in death; nor any kind of spiritual coming, as to its first meaning, at any rate. I am persuaded that the clear run of the words involves our Lord's coming, in his second advent, when he will come to receive, not you or me as individuals who, one by one, will enter into rest, but to receive his whole Church into the place which he shall then have prepared for her. After the resurrection, you must remember, we shall need a place to live in – a literal, material place of abode, for this body of ours will be alive as well as our spirit, and it will need a world to live in, a new heaven and a new earth.

I am not going to enter into any speculations about the matter, but it seems to me clear enough, in this, text, that Christ is preparing a place somewhere not for disembodied spirits, for they are already before the throne of God perfectly blest, but for the entire manhood of his people, when spirit, soul and body shall be again united, and the complete man shall receive the adoption, to wit, the redemption of the body, and the whole manhood of every believer shall be perfected in the glory of Christ.

I do not know what better world, in many respects, there could be than this, so far as material nature is concerned; it is so full of the beauty and loveliness that God pours upon it on every side; it is a wonderful world –

> Where every prospect pleases,
> And only man is vile –

but I could not reconcile myself to the idea that this world would be heaven. No; my thoughts rise far above the loftiest hills, the most flowery meads, the rolling ocean, and the flowing rivers. Earth has not space enough to be our heaven. She has too narrow a bound, and she is too coarse a thing, bright gem though she is, for perfected manhood to possess throughout eternity. It will do well enough for the thousand years of glory, if it shall literally be that we shall reign with Christ upon it during the millennial age; but it is a drossy thing, and if it ever is to be the scene of the new heavens and the new earth, it must first pass through the fire. The very smell of sin is upon it; and God will not use this globe as a vessel unto honour until he has purified it with fire as once he did with water; and then, mayhap, it may serve for this higher purpose; but I scarcely think it will.

Even now, Jesus is preparing, and has gone away on purpose to prepare a place for us; and he will come again, 'with the voice of the archangel, and with the trump of God,' and he will catch his people away, and will bear them to the eternal home where their felicity shall know no end. That is what I suppose to be the meaning of our Lord's words. 'But', perhaps you say to me, 'what do you mean by what you have been saying?' I reply, I do not know to the full; I can but dimly guess at the meaning of what my Lord has said – that he is doing something so glorious for *all* his people that, perhaps, if I did know it, I might not be allowed to tell you; for there are some things which, when a man knows them, it is not lawful for him to utter. Did not Paul see a great deal when he was caught up into paradise? Yet he has told us very little about it; for there was a finger laid upon his lip that bade him know it for himself, but not to tell it to others. 'Eye hath not seen, nor ear heard, neither have entered into the heart of man, the things which God hath prepared for them that love him;' and though he has 'revealed them unto us by his Spirit', even the Spirit who searcheth the deep things of God, yet it is not possible for us to tell all that has been revealed to us.

It strikes me that there is some little light to be obtained concerning this preparation of heaven by Christ, if I leave the direct and literal meaning of the words, and think of the future state as a whole rather than in detail. Do you not think, dear friends, that *our Lord Jesus Christ prepares heaven for his people by going there?* I mean this. Supposing you were to be lifted up to a state which was looked upon as heavenly, but if Jesus was not there, it would be no heaven to you. But wherever I may go, when I do go, if Jesus is already there, I do not care where it is. Wherever he is shall be my heaven; for, as I said in the reading, that is our very first and last thought about heaven, to be with Christ where he is. To be with Christ is far better than to be anywhere else.

Well, then, the first thing that Christ had to do, in order to prepare heaven for his people, was to go to heaven, for that made it heaven. Then were heaven's lamps kindled; then did heaven's heralds ring out their supernal melodies; then did the whole of the New Jerusalem seem to be ablaze with a glory brighter than the sun, for 'the Lamb is the light thereof.' When he comes there, then all is bliss. Do you not see, beloved, that he has prepared heaven by going there? His being there will make it heaven for you, so you need not begin asking what else there will be in heaven. There will be all manner of rare delights to spiritual men, but the chief of them all will be that Jesus is there. As Rowland Hill used to sing, so may you and I comfort ourselves with this thought –

> And this I do find – we two are so joined –
> He'll not be in glory, and leave me behind.

If I may but be where he is, that shall be heaven to me.

But another reflection is this: that *our Lord Jesus Christ has prepared heaven for his people by the merit of his atonement.*

Thus hath he opened the kingdom of heaven to all believers. He rent the veil and made a way into the holiest of all for all who trust him; but, in addition to that, he perfumed heaven with the fragrance of his sacrifice. If heaven be the place of the Godhead, as we know it is, we could not have stood there without the Mediator. If heaven be the throne of the great King, we could not have stood there without the cloud of perfumed incense from Christ's meritorious death and righteousness ever rising up before that throne. But, now, heaven is a safe place for the saints to enter.

Now may they tread that sea of glass, like as of fire; and know that it is glass, and that no fire from it will consume them. Now will they be able to come up near to God, and not be afraid. I quote again a passage that often leaps to my lips, a text of Scripture which is often shamefully misused: 'Who among us shall dwell with the devouring fire? Who among us shall dwell with everlasting burnings?' Why, none of us could so dwell unless Christ had changed us by his grace; but now we may do so.

What is the Scriptural answer to those questions, 'Who among us shall dwell with the devouring fire? Who among us shall dwell with everlasting burnings?' What saith the Scripture? Listen: 'He that walketh righteously, and speaketh uprightly; he that despiseth the gain of oppressions; that shaketh his hands from holding of bribes, that stoppeth his ears from hearing of blood; and shutteth his eyes from seeing evils. He shall dwell on high: his place of defence shall be the munitions of rocks: bread shall be given him; his waters shall be sure. Thine eyes shall see the King in his beauty: they shall behold the land that is very far off.'

This is the man who shall dwell there. With God, who is a consuming fire, we, like the holy children in the burning, fiery furnace, shall find it safe to dwell, and find it bliss to dwell, because Christ is there. But there would have been no heaven, in the presence of God, for any man that lives, after sin had once come into the world, if Jesus had not gone there as the high priest of old went up to the blazing throne whereon the Shekinah shone, and sprinkled it with blood out of the basin, and then waved the censer to and fro till the thick smoke hid the cherubim, and, for a while resting, spake with God. Even so, has Christ gone within the veil, and sprinkled his own atoning blood upon his Father's throne, and then waved aloft the censer full of the incense of his mercy; and now it is safe for us to have access with boldness to the throne of glory as well as to the throne of grace. Thus hath he prepared a place for us.

Another meaning, I think, is allowable, namely, that *Christ has prepared heaven for us by appearing there in his glory.* I said that his very presence made heaven, but now I add that his glory there makes heaven yet more glorious. How does Christ describe the heavenly state? 'Father, I will that they also, whom thou hast given me, be with me where I am; that they may behold my glory.' It will be their bliss, then, to see his glory; but there would have been no glory for them to see if he had not gone there in his glory. But, now, his presence there, in all his majesty and splendour, makes heaven still more glorious.

Oh, how I long to see him in his glory! Long to see him, did I say? I would part with all the joys of time and sense to gaze upon him seated upon his throne. Oh! what will it be to see him? You have seen how painters have failed when they have tried to depict him. The bravest artist may well tremble, and the brightest colours fade, when anyone tries to paint him even in his humiliation. There is no other face so marred as his face was; but what will it be in heaven when it is marred no more? No tear in his eye! No spittle running down his cheeks! No giving of his face to them that pluck out the hair; but, oh, the glory of manhood perfected and allied with Deity! 'The King in his beauty!' Why, methinks, to see him but for a minute, if we never saw him again, might furnish us with an eternity of bliss; but we shall gaze upon him, in his glory, day without night, never fainting, or flagging, or tiring, but delighting for ever to behold him smile, for evermore to call him ours, and to see him still before us. He has gone to heaven, then, in his glory and, surely, that is preparing a place for us!

Besides that, we cannot tell what arrangements had to be made in order to prepare a place of eternal blessedness for the Lord's redeemed. Certain it is that, in the economy of the universe, everything has its place. Men have discovered, as you know, what they call evolution. They think that one thing grows out of another, because long before they were born everybody with half an eye could see that one thing fitted into another; and as one step rises above another step by a beautiful gradation, so do the created things of God. Not that they grow out of each other any more than the stones of a staircase grow out of one another; they rise above each other, but they were so made from the first by the skill and wisdom of God. That a dewdrop should be precisely of the size and shape that it is, is necessary to the perfection of the universe. That there should be insects born in such a month to fertilize the flowers that bloom in that month, and others to suck the sweetness of those flowers, is all necessary. God has arranged everything, from the little to the great, with perfect skill. There is a place for everything with God, and everything in its place.

It was a question where to put man. He had a place once. When God created this world, he made a pyramid and set man upon the very top of it, giving him dominion over all the works of his hands; but then man fell. Now, it is more difficult to restore than it is at first to place. Often and often, you must have found that, when a thing has gone awry, it has cost you more trouble to set it right than if it had to be made *de novo*. Where, then, was the place for man to be? O matchless love, O sacred wisdom, that provided that man's place should be where Christ's place was and is! Lo, he who came down from heaven, and who also was in heaven, has gone back to heaven. He carried manhood with him; and, in so doing, one with him, his Church has found her place. His union to the Godhead has found a place for his Church at the right hand of God, even the Father, where Christ sitteth; and all is as it should be.

As I have already told you, I do not know much about this matter; but I should not wonder if there has been going on, ever since Christ went up to heaven, a putting things straight – getting this race of creatures into its proper place, and that other race, and the other race; so that, when we get to heaven, nobody will say, 'You have got my place.' Not even Gabriel will say to me, 'Why, what business have you here? You have got my place.' No, no; you shall have a place of your own, beloved; and all the members of Christ's Church shall find a place prepared which no one else shall be able to claim, for nobody shall be dispossessed or put out of his rightful position.

It struck me, as I turned this subject over in my mind, that *our Lord Jesus Christ knew that there was a place to be prepared for each one of his people.* It may be – I cannot tell – that in some part of the society of heaven, one spirit will be happier than it might have been in another part. You know that, even though you love all the brethren, you cannot help feeling most at home with some of them. Our blessed Lord and Master had no sinful favouritism, yet he did love twelve men better than all the rest of his disciples; and out of the twelve he loved three, whom he introduced into mysteries from which he excluded the other nine; and even out of the three, there was one, you know, who was 'that disciple whom Jesus loved'. Now, everybody here has his likings; I do not know if we shall carry anything of that spirit to heaven. If we do, Christ has so prepared a place for us that you shall be nearest, in your position and occupation, to those who would contribute most to your happiness. You shall be where you can most honour God, and most enjoy God. You would be glad enough to be anywhere, would you not? – with the very least of the saints in heaven if there 'be any degrees of glory' among their thrones, or at his feet, as long as you might see Christ's face.

But, depend upon it, if there be any association – any more intimate connection – between some saints than among others, Jesus Christ will so beautifully arrange it that we shall all be in the happiest places. If you were to give a dinner-party, and you had a number of friends there, you would like to pick the seats for them. You would say, 'Now, there is So-and-so, I know that he would like to sit next to So-and-so'; and you would try so to arrange it. Well, in that grand wedding feast above, our Saviour has so prepared a place for us that he will find us each the right position. I was talking, this afternoon, with one whom I very dearly love, and she said to me, 'I hope my place in heaven will not be far off yours'; and I replied, 'Well, I trust so, too; but we are not married or given in marriage there.' Such ties and such relationships must end, as far as they are after the flesh; but we know that there have been bonds of spirit that may still continue.

I sometimes think that, if I could have any choice as to those I should live near in heaven, I should like to live in the region of such queer folk as Rowland Hill and John Berridge. I think I should get on best with them, for we could talk together of the way wherein God led us; and of how he brought souls to Christ by us, though some said that we were a deal too merry when we were down below, and that the people laughed when they listened to us, and some spoke as if that were a great sin. We will make them laugh up yonder, I warrant you; as we tell again the wonders of redeeming love, and of the grace of God, their mouths shall be filled with laughter and their tongues with singing; and then, –

> Loudest of the crowd I'll sing,
> While heaven's resounding mansions ring
> With shouts of sovereign grace…

and I expect each of you, who love the Lord, will say the same.

I have no time for the other part of the sermon. You must come again to hear about *the prepared people*. But let me just say this to you. The place is prepared, are you prepared for it? Dost thou believe on the Lord Jesus Christ? If so, your preparation has begun. Dost thou love the Lord and love his people? If so, thy preparation is going on. Dost thou hate sin and dost thou pant after holiness. If so, thy preparation is progressing. Art thou nothing at all and is Jesus Christ thine All-in-all? Then thou art almost ready and may the Lord keep thee in that condition; and before long, swing up the gates of pearl and let thee in to the prepared place!

May the Lord bring us all safely there, for Jesus' sake! Amen.

2

Heavenly Rest[1]

There remaineth therefore a rest to the people of God.
Hebrews 4:9

The Apostle proved, in the former part of this and the latter part of the preceding chapter, that there was a rest promised in Scripture called the rest of God. He proved that Israel did not attain that rest for God sware in his wrath, saying, 'They shall not enter into my rest.' He proved that this did not merely refer to the rest of the land of Canaan; for he says that after they were in Canaan,

---

1.   A sermon delivered on Sunday morning, 24 May 1857, at the Music Hall, Royal Surrey Gardens, London.

David himself speaks again in after ages concerning the rest of God, as a thing which was yet to come. Again he proves that 'seeing those to whom it was promised did not enter in, because of unbelief, and it remaineth that some must enter in, therefore,' saith he, 'there remaineth a rest to the people of God.'

'*My* rest', says God: the rest of God! Something more wonderful than any other kind of rest. In my text, it is (in the original) called the *Sabbatism* – not the Sabbath, but the rest of the Sabbath – not the outward ritual of the Sabbath, which was binding upon the Jew, but the inward spirit of the Sabbath, which is the joy and delight of the Christian. 'There remaineth therefore' – because others have not had it, because some are to have it – 'There remaineth therefore a rest to the people of God.'

Now, this rest, I believe, is partly enjoyed on earth. 'We that have believed do enter into rest,' for we have ceased from our own works, as God did from his. But the full fruition and rich enjoyment of it remains in the future and eternal state of the beatified on the other side the stream of death. Of that it shall be our delightful work to talk a little this morning. And oh! If God should help me to raise but one of his feeble saints on the wings of love to look within the veil, and see the joys of the future, I shall be well contented to have made the joy-bells ring in one heart at least, to have set one eye flashing with joy, and to have made one spirit light with gladness.

The rest of heaven! I shall try first to *exhibit it* and then to *extol it*.

First, I shall try to *exhibit* the rest of heaven; and in doing so I shall exhibit it, first by way of contrast, and then by way of comparison.

To begin then, I shall try to exhibit heaven *by way of contrast*. The rest of the righteous in glory is now to be contrasted with certain other things. We will contrast it, first, *with the best estate of the worldling and the sinner*. The worldling has frequently a good estate. Sometimes his vats overflow, his barns are crammed, his heart is full of joy and gladness, there are periods with him when he flourishes like a green bay tree, when field is added to field, and house to house, when he pulls down his barns and builds greater, when the river of his joy is full, and the ocean of his life is at its flood with joy and blessedness.

But oh beloved, the state of the righteous up there is not for a moment to be compared with the joy of the sinner; − it is so infinitely superior, so far surpassing it, that it seems impossible that I should even try to set it in contrast. The worldling, when his corn and his wine are increased, has a glad eye and a joyous heart; but even then he has the direful thought that *he may soon leave his wealth*. He remembers that death may cut him down, that he must then leave all his fair riches behind him, and sleep like the meanest of the land in a narrow coffin, six feet of earth his only heritage. Not so the righteous man: he has obtained an inheritance which is 'undefiled, and that fadeth not away.' He knows that there is no possibility of his losing his joys:

> He is securely blessed,
> Has done with sin, and care, and woe,
> And doth with Jesus rest.

He has no dread of dissolution, no fear of the coffin or the shroud, and so far the life of heaven is not worthy to be put in comparison with the life of the sinner.

But the worldling, with all his joys, always has *a worm at the root* of them. Ye votaries of pleasure! the blush upon your cheek is frequently but a painted deception. Ah! ye sons and daughters of gaiety! the light foot of your dance is not in keeping with the heavy woe of your miserable spirits. Do you not confess that if by the excitement of company you for awhile forget the emptiness of your heart, yet silence, and the hour of midnight, and the waking watches of your bed, bid you sometimes think that there must be something more blessed than the mere wanderings of gaiety in which you now are found?

You are trying the world some of you; speak then! Do you not find it empty? Might it not be said of the world, as an old philosopher said of it when he represented a man with it in his hands smiting it and listening to its ringing? Touch it, touch it I make it ring again; it is empty. So it is with the world. You know it is so; and if you know it not as yet, the day is coming when after you have plucked the sweets you shall be pricked with the thorn, and when you shall find that all is unsatisfactory that does not begin and end with God. Not so the Christian in heaven. For him there are no nights; and if there be times of solitude and rest, he is ever filled with ecstatic joy. His river floweth ever full of bliss, without one pebble of sorrow over which it ripples, he has no aching conscience, no 'aching void the world can never fill'. He is supremely blessed, satisfied with favour, and full with the goodness of the Lord.

And ye know, ye worldlings, that your best estates often bring you great anxiety, *lest they should depart from you.* You are not so foolish yet as to conceive that riches endure for ever. You men of business are frequently led to see that riches take to themselves wings and fly away. You have accumulated a fortune; but you find it is harder to retain than it is to get. You are seeking after a competence; but you find that you grasp at shadows that flit away — that the everlasting vicissitudes of business and the constant changes of mankind are causes of prudent alarm to you, for you fear that you shall lose your gods, and that your gourd shall be eaten by the worm, and fall down, and your shadow shall be taken away. Not so the Christian. He lives in a house that can never hasten to decay; he wears a crown, the glister of which shall never be dim; he has a garment which shall never wax old; he has bliss that never can depart from him, nor he from it. He is now firmly set, like a pillar of marble in the temple of God. The world may rock, the tempest may sway it like the cradle of a child; but there, above the world, above the perpetual revolution of the stars, the Christian stands secure and immovable; trio rest infinitely surpasseth yours.

Ah! ye shall go to all the fabled luxuries of eastern monarchs, and see their dainty couches and their luscious wines. Behold the riches of their pleasantry! How charming is the music that lulls them to their sleep! How gently moves the fan that wafts them to their slumber! But ah!

> I would not change my blest estate
> For all the world calls good or great;
> And whilst my faith can keep her hold
> I envy not the sinner's gold —

I reckon that the richest, highest, noblest condition of a worldly man is not worthy to be compared with the joy that is to be revealed hereafter in the breasts of those who are sanctified. O ye spendthrift mortals, that for one merry dance and a giddy life will lose a world of joys! O fools that catch at bubbles and lose realities! O ten thousand times mad men, that grasp at shadows and lose the substance! What! sirs, do you think a little round of pleasure, a few years of gaiety and merriment, just a little time of the tossing about, to and fro, of worldly business, is a compensation for eternal ages of unfading bliss! Oh! how foolish will you conceive yourselves to be, when you are in the next state, when cast away from heaven you will see the saints blessed! I think I hear your mournful soliloquy, 'Oh! How cheaply did I sell my soul! What a poor price did I get for all I have now lost! I have lost the palace and the crown, and the joy and bliss for ever, and am shut up in hell! And for what did I lose it? I lost it for the lascivious wanton kiss. I lost it for the merry drunken song; I lost it for just a few short years of pleasures, which, after all, were only painted pleasures!' Oh! I think I see you in your lost estates, cursing yourselves, rending your hair, that you should have sold heaven for counters and have changed away eternal life for pitiful farthings, which were spent quickly and which burned your hand in the spending of them! Oh! that ye were wise, that ye would weigh those things, and reckon that a life of the greatest happiness here is nothing compared with the glorious hereafter: 'There remaineth a rest to the people of God.'

Now let me put it in *more pleasing contrast*. I shall contrast the rest of the believer above with the miserable estate of the believer sometimes here below. Christians have their sorrows. Suns have their spots, skies have their clouds, and Christians have their sorrows too. But oh! how different will the state of the righteous be up there, from the state of the believer here!

Here the Christian has to suffer anxiety. He is anxious to serve his Master, to do his best in his day and generation.

His constant cry is, 'Help me to serve thee, O my God,' and he looks out, day after day, with a strong desire for opportunities of doing good. Ah! if he be an active Christian, he will have much labour, much toil, in endeavouring to serve his Master; and there will be times when he will say, 'My soul is in haste to be gone; I am not wearied *of* the labour, I am wearied *in* it. To toil thus in the sun, though for a good Master, is not the thing that just now I desire.'

Ah! Christian, the day shall soon be over, and thou shalt no longer have to toil; the sun is nearing the horizon; it shall rise again with a brighter day than thou hast ever seen before. There, up in heaven, Luther has no more to face a thundering Vatican; Paul has no more to run from city to city, and continent to continent; there Baxter has no more to toil in his pulpit, to preach with a broken heart to hard-hearted sinners; there no longer has Knox to 'cry aloud and spare not' against the immoralities of the false church; there no more shall be the strained lung, and the tired throat, and the aching eye; no more shall the Sunday school teacher feel that his Sabbath is a day of joyful weariness; no more shall the tract distributor meet with rebuffs. No, there, those who have served their country and their God, those who have toiled for man's welfare, with all their might, shall enter into everlasting rest. Sheathed is the sword, the banner is furled, the fight is over, the victory won; and they rest from their labours.

Here, too, the Christian is always *sailing onward*, he is always in motion, he feels that he has not yet attained. Like Paul he can say, 'Forgetting the things that are behind, I press forward to that which is before.' But there his weary head shall be crowned with unfading light. There the ship that has been speeding onward shall furl its sails in the port of eternal bliss. There he who, like an arrow, has sped his way shall be fixed for ever in the target. There we who like fleeting clouds were driven by every wind, shall gently distil in one perennial shower of everlasting joy. There is no progress, no motion there; they are at rest, they have attained the summit of the mountain, they have ascended to their God and our God. Higher they cannot go; they have reached the *ultima Thule*, there are no fortunate islands beyond; this is life's utmost end of happiness; and they furl their sails, rest from their labours, and enjoy themselves for aye. There is a difference between the progress of earth and the perfect fixity of the rest of heaven.

Here, too, the believer is often the subject of *doubt and fear*. 'Am I his or am I not?' is often the cry. He trembleth lest he should be deceived, at times he almost despairs, and is inclined not to put his name down as one of the children of God. Dark insinuations are whispered into his ears, he thinks that God's mercy is clean gone for ever, and that he will not be mindful of him any more. Again, his sins sometimes upbraid him, and he thinks God will not have mercy on him. He has a poor, fainting heart; he is like Ready-to-halt, he has to go all his way on crutches; he has a poor feeble mind, always tumbling down over a straw, and fearing one day he shall be drowned in a cart-rut. Though the lions are chained, he is as much afraid of them as if they were loose. The hill called Difficulty often afrights him; going down into the valley of humiliation is often troublesome work to him; but there, there are no hills to climb, no dragons to fight, no foes to conquer, no dangers to dread. Ready-to-halt, when he dies, will bury his crutches, and Feeble-mind will leave his feebleness behind him; Fearing will never fear again; poor Doubting-heart will learn confidently to believe.

Oh, joy above all joys! The day is coming when I shall 'know as I am known', when I shall not want to ask whether I am his or not, for in his arms encircled, there shall be no room for doubt. Oh! Christian, you think there are slips between your lips and that cup of joy, but when you grasp the handle of that cup with your hand, and are drinking draughts of ineffable delight, then you will have no doubt or fear.

> There you shall see his face,
> And never, never sin
> There from the rivers of his grace,
> Drink endless pleasures in.

Here, too, on earth, the Christian has to *suffer*; here he has the aching head and the pained body; his limbs may be bruised or broken, disease may rack him with torture; he may be an afflicted one from his birth, he may have lost an eye or an ear or he may have lost many of his powers; or if not, being of a weakly constitution he may have to spend the most of his days and nights upon the bed of weariness. Or if his body be sound, yet what suffering he has in his mind! Conflicts between depravity and gross temptations from the evil one, assaults of hell, perpetual attacks of divers kinds, from the world, the flesh and the devil. But there, no aching head, no weary heart; there no palsied arm, no brow ploughed with the furrows of old age; there the lost limb shall be recovered, and old age shall find itself endowed with perpetual youth; there the infirmities of the flesh shall be left behind, given to the worm and devoured by corruption. There they shall flit, as on the wings of angels, from pole to pole, and from place to place, without weariness or anguish; there they shall never need to lie upon the bed of rest, or the bed of suffering, for day without night, with joy unflagging, they shall circle God's throne rejoicing, and ever praise Him who hath said, 'The inhabitants there shall never be sick.'

There, too, they shall be free from *persecution*. Here, Sicilian Vespers and St Bartholomew and Smithfield are well-known words; but there shall be none to taunt them with a cruel word, or touch them with a cruel hand. There, emperors and kings are not known, and those who had power to torture them cease to be. They are in the society of saints; they shall be free from all the idle converse of the wicked, and from their cruel jeers set free for ever. Set free from persecution! Ye army of martyrs, ye were slain, ye were torn asunder, ye were cast to wild beasts, ye wandered about in sheep skins and goats' skins, destitute, afflicted and tormented. I see you now, a mighty host. The habiliments you wear are torn with thorns; your faces are scarred with sufferings; I see you at your stakes, and on your crosses; I hear your words of submission on your racks, I see you in your prisons, I behold you in your pillories – but

> Now ye are arrayed in white,
> Brighter than the noonday-sun;
> Fairest of the sons of light,
> Nearest the eternal throne.

These are they who 'for their Master died, who love the cross and crown'; they waded through seas of blood, in order to obtain the inheritance; and there they are, with the blood-red crown of martyrdom about their heads, that ruby brightness, far excelling every other. Yes, there is no persecution there. 'There remaineth a rest for the people of God.'

Alas! in this mortal state the child of God is also subject to *sin*; even he faileth in his duty, and wandereth from his God; even he doth not walk in all the law of his God blameless, though he desireth to do it. Sin now troubleth him constantly; but there sin is dead, there they have no temptation to sin, from without or from within, but they are perfectly free to serve their Master. Here the child of God has sometimes to weep repentingly of his backslidings; but there they never shed tears of penitence, for they have never cause to do so.

And last of all, here, the child of God has to wet the cold ashes of his relatives with *tears*; here he has to bid adieu to all that is lovely and fair of mortal race; here it is he hears, 'earth to earth, and dust to dust, and ashes to ashes', while the solemn music of the dust upon the coffin lid beats doleful time to those words. Here is the mother buried, the child snatched away, the husband rent from the bosom of a loving wife, the brother parted from the sister. The plate upon the coffin, the last coat of arms of earth, earth's last emblems are here ever before our eyes. But there never once shall be heard the toll of the funeral bell, no hearse with plumes has ever darkened the streets of gold, no emblems of sorrow have ever intruded into the homes of the immortal, they are strangers to the meaning of death; they cannot die – they live for ever, having no power to decay, and no possibility of corruption. Oh! rest of the righteous, how blest art thou, where families shall again be bound up in one bundle, where parted friends shall again meet to part no more, and where the whole Church of Christ united in one mighty circle, shall together praise God and the Lamb throughout eternal ages.

Brethren, I have tried thus to set the rest of the righteous in the way of contrast; I feel I have failed. Poor are the

words I can utter to tell you of immortal things. Even holy
Baxter himself, when he wrote of the 'Saints' Rest,' paused
and said: 'But these are only tinklings compared with the
full thunders of heaven.' I cannot tell you, dear friends, nor
can mortal tell, what God hath prepared for them that love
him.

And now I shall try very briefly to exhibit this contrast *in
the way of comparison.* The Christian hath some rest here, but
nothing compared with the rest which is to come.

There is the *rest of the Church.* When the believer joins
the Church of God, and becomes united with them, he
may expect to rest. The good old writer of *The Pilgrim's
Progress* says that when the weary pilgrims were once
admitted to the House Beautiful, they were shown to sleep
in a chamber called 'peace', or 'rest'. The church member at
the Lord's table has a sweet enjoyment of rest in fellowship
with the saints; but ah! up there the rest of church
fellowship far surpasses anything that is known here; for
there are no divisions there, no angry words at the church
meetings, no harsh thoughts of one another, no bickerings
about doctrine, no fightings about practice. There Baptist
and Presbyterian and Independent and Wesleyan and
Episcopalian, serving the same Lord, and having been
washed in the same blood, sing the same song, and are all
joined in one. There pastors and deacons never look coolly
on each other; no haughty prelates there, no lofty-minded
ministers there, but all meek and lowly, all knit together in
brotherhood; they have a rest which surpasseth all the rest
of the Church on earth.

There is, again, a rest of *faith* which a Christian enjoys;
a sweet rest. Many of us have known it. We have known

what it is, when the billows of trouble have run high, to hide ourselves in the breast of Christ, and feel secure. We have cast our anchor deep into the rocks of God's promise; we have gone to sleep in our chamber and have not feared the tempest; we have looked at tribulation, and have smiled; we have looked at death himself, and have laughed him to scorn; we have had such trust by Christian faith that, dauntless and fearless, nothing could move us. Yes, in the midst of calumny, reproach, slander and contempt, we have said, 'I shall not be moved, for God is on my side.' But the rest up there is better still, more unruffled, more sweet, more perfectly calm, more enduring and more lasting than even the rest of faith.

And, again, the Christian sometimes has the blessed rest of *communion*. There are happy moments when he puts his head on the Saviour's breast – when, like John, he feels that he is close to the Saviour's heart, and there he sleeps. 'God giveth his beloved sleep'; not the sleep of unconsciousness, but the sleep of joy. Happy, happy, happy are the dreams we have had on the couch of communion; blessed have been the times, when, like the spouse in Solomon's song, we could say of Christ, 'His left hand was under my head, and with his right hand did he embrace me.'

> But sweeter still the fountain head,
> Though sweet may be the stream.

When we shall have plunged into a very bath of joy, we shall have found the delights even of communion on earth to have been but the dipping of the finger in the cup, but the dipping of the bread in the dish, whereas heaven itself shall be the participation of the whole of the joy, and not the mere antepast of it. Here we sometimes enter into the portico of happiness, there we shall go into the presence chamber of the King; here we look over the hedge and see the flowers in heaven's garden, there we shall walk between the beds of bliss, and pluck fresh flowers at each step; here we just look and see the sunlight of heaven in the distance, like the lamps of the thousand-gated cities shining afar off, but there we shall see them in all their blaze of splendour; here we listen to the whisperings of heaven's melody, borne by winds from afar, but there, entranced, amidst the grand oratorio of the blessed, we shall join in the everlasting hallelujah to the great Messiah, the God, the I AM. Oh! again I say, do we not wish to mount aloft, and fly away, to enter into the rest which remaineth to the people of God?

And now, yet more briefly, and then we shall have done. I am to endeavour to *extol* this rest, as I have tried to *exhibit* it. I would extol this rest for many reasons; and oh! that I were eloquent, that I might extol it as it deserves! Oh! for the lip of angel, and the burning tongue of cherub, to talk now of the bliss of the sanctified and of the rest of God's people!

It is, first, a *perfect* rest. They are wholly at rest in heaven. Here rest is but partial. I hope in a little time to cease from everyday labours for a season, but then the head will think, and the mind may be looking forward to prospective labour, and whilst the body is still, the brain will yet be in motion. Here, on Sabbath days a vast multitude of you sit in God's house, but many of you are obliged to stand, and rest but little except in your mind, and even when the mind is at rest the body is wearied with the toil of standing. You have a weary mile, perhaps many miles, to go to your homes on the Sabbath day. And let the Sabbatarian say what he will, you may work on the Sabbath day, if you work for God; and this Sabbath day's work of going to the house of God is work for God, and God accepts it. For yourselves you may not labour. God commands you to rest, but if you have to toil these three, these four, these five, these six miles, as many of you have done, I will not and I must not blame you. 'The priests in the sanctuary profane the Sabbath, and are blameless.' It is toil and labour, it is true, but it is for a good cause − for your Master.

But there, my friends, the rest is perfect; the body there rests perpetually, the mind too always rests; though the inhabitants are always busy, always serving God, yet they are never weary, never toil-worn, never fagged; they never fling themselves upon their couches at the end of the day, and cry, 'Oh! when shall I be away from this land of toil?' They never stand up in the burning sunlight, and wipe the hot sweat from their brow; they never rise from their bed in the morning, half refreshed, to go to laborious study. No, they are perfectly at rest, stretched on the couch of eternal joy. They know not the semblance of a tear; they have done with sin, and care, and woe, and with their Saviour rest.

Again, it is a *seasonable* rest. How seasonable it will be for some of you! Ye sons of wealth, ye know not the toils of the poor; the horny-handed labourer, perhaps, you have not seen, and you not how he has to tug and to toil. Among my congregation I have many of a class upon whom I have always looked with pity, poor women who must rise tomorrow morning with the sun, and begin that everlasting 'stitch, stitch', that works their finger to the bone. And from Monday morning till Saturday night, many of you, my members, and multitudes of you, my hearers, will not be able to lay aside your needle and your thread, except when, tired and weary, you fall back on your chair, and are lulled to sleep by your thoughts of labour! Oh! how seasonable will heaven's rest be to you! Oh! how glad will you be, when you get there, to find that there are no Monday mornings, no more toil for you, but rest, eternal rest!

Others of you have hard manual labour to perform; you have reason to thank God that you are strong enough to do it and you are not ashamed of your work; for labour is an honour to a man. But still there are times when you say, 'I wish I were not so dragged to death by the business of London life.' We have but little rest in this huge city, our day is longer, and our work is harder than our friends in the country. You have sometimes sighed to go into the green fields for a breath of fresh air; you have longed to hear the song of the sweet birds that used to wake you when you were lads; you have regretted the bright blue sky, the beauteous flowers, and the thousand charms of a country life. And perhaps, you will never get beyond this smoky city, but remember, when you get up there, 'sweet fields arrayed in living green' and 'rivers of delight' shall be the place where you shall rest; you shall have all the joys you can conceive of in that home of happiness; and though worn and weary, you come to your grave, tottering on your staff, having journeyed through the wilderness of life, like a weary camel, which has only stopped on the Sabbath to sip its little water at the well, or to be baited at the oasis, there you will arrive at your journey's end, laden with gold and spices, and enter into the grand caravanserai of heaven, and enjoy for ever the things you have wearily carried with you here.

And I must say, that to others of us who have not to toil with our hands, heaven will be a seasonable rest. Those of us who have to tire our brain day after day will find it no slight boon to have an everlasting rest above. I will not boast of what I may do; there may be many who do more, there may be many who are perpetually and daily striving to serve God, and are using their mind's best energies in so doing. But this much I may say, that almost every week I have the pleasure of preaching twelve times, and often in my sleep do I think of what I shall say next time. Not having the advantage of laying out my seven shillings and sixpence in buying manuscripts, it costs me hard, diligent labour to find even something to say. And I sometimes have a difficulty to keep the hopper full in the mill. I feel that if I had not now and then a rest I should have no wheat for God's children.

Still it is on, on, on and on we must go. We hear the chariot wheels of God behind us, and we dare not stop; we think that eternity is drawing nigh, and we must go on. Rest to us now is more than labour, we want to be at work; but oh! how seasonable it shall be, when to the minister it shall be said –

> Servant of God, well done!
> Rest from thy loved employ;
> The battle fought, the victory won,
> Enter thy Master's joy.

It will be seasonable rest. You that are weary with state cares, and have had to learn the ingratitude of men; you that have sought honours, and have got them to your cost; you seek to do your best, but your very independence of spirit is called servility, whilst your servility would have been praised! You who seek to honour God, and not to honour men, who will not bind yourselves to parties, but seek in your own independent and honest judgment to serve your country and your God, you, I say, when God shall see fit to call you to himself, will find it no small joy to have done with parliaments, to have done with states and kingdoms, and to have laid aside your honours, to receive honours more lasting amongst those who dwell for ever before the throne of the Most High.

This rest, my brethren, ought to be extolled, because it is *eternal*. Here my best joys bear 'mortal' on their brow; here my fair flowers fade; here my sweet cups have dregs and are soon empty; here my sweetest birds must die, and their melody must soon be hushed; here my most pleasant days must have their nights; here the flowings of my bliss must have their ebbs; everything doth pass away, but there everything shall be immortal; the harp shall be unrusted, the crown unwithered, the eye undimmed, the voice unfaltering, the heart unwavering, and the being wholly consolidated unto eternity. Happy day, happy day, when mortality shall be swallowed up of life, and the mortal shall have put on immortality!

And then, lastly, this glorious rest is to be best of all commended for its *certainty*. 'There remaineth a rest to the people of God.' Doubting one, thou hast often said, 'I fear I shall never enter heaven.' Fear not, all the people of God shall enter there; there is no fear about it. I love the quaint saying of a dying man, who, in his country brogue, exclaimed, 'I have no fear of going home; I have sent all before me. God's finger is on the latch of my door and I am ready for him to enter.' 'But', said one, 'are you not afraid least you should miss your inheritance?' 'Nay,' said he, 'nay. There is one crown in heaven that the angel Gabriel could not wear; it will fit no head but mine. There is one throne in heaven that Paul the Apostle could not fill; it was made for me, and I shall have it. There is one dish at the banquet that I must eat, or else it will be untasted, for God has set it apart for me.'

O Christian, what a joyous thought! Thy portion is secure! 'There remaineth a rest.' 'But cannot I forfeit it?' No, it is entailed. If I be a child of God I shall not lose it. It is mine as securely as if I were there.

> Come, Christian, mount to Pisgah's top,
> And view the landscape o'er.

Seest thou that little river of death, glistening in the sunlight, and across it dost thou see the pinnacles of the eternal city? Dost thou mark the pleasant suburbs and all the joyous inhabitants? Turn thine eye to that spot. Dost thou see where that ray of light is glancing now? There is a little spot there; dost thou see it? That is thy patrimony; that is thine. Oh, if thou couldst fly across thou wouldst see written upon it, 'This remaineth for such an one, preserved for him only. He shall be caught up and dwell for ever with God.'

Poor doubting one; see thine inheritance; it is thine. If thou believest in the Lord Jesus, thou art one of the Lord's people; if thou hast repented of sin, thou art one of the Lord's people; if thou hast been renewed in heart, thou art one of the Lord's people, and there is a place for thee, a crown for thee, a harp for thee. No one else shall have it but thyself, and thou shalt have it ere long.

Just pardon me one moment if I beg of you to conceive of yourselves as being in heaven. Is it not a strange thing to think of – a poor clown in heaven? Think, how will you feel with your crown on your head? Weary matron, many years have rolled over you. How changed will be the scene when you are young again! Ah, toil-worn labourer, only think when thou shalt rest for aye. Canst thou conceive it? Couldst thou but think for a moment of thyself as being in heaven now, what a strange surprise would seize thee! Thou wouldst not so as much say, 'What! are these streets of gold? What! are these walls of jasper? What, am I here? In white? Am I here, with a crown on my brow? Am I here singing, that was always groaning? What! I praise God that once cursed him? What! I lifting up my voice in his honour? Oh, precious blood that washed me clean! Oh, precious faith that set me free! Oh, precious Spirit that made me repent, else I had been cast away and been in hell! But oh! what wonders! Angels! I am surprised. I am enraptured! Wonder of wonders! Oh! gates of pearls, I long since heard of you! Oh! joys that never fade, I long since heard tell of you! But I am like the Queen of Sheba, the half has not yet been told me. Profusion, oh profusion of bliss! – wonder of wonders! – miracle of miracles! What a world I am in! And oh! that I am here, this is the topmost miracle of all!'

And yet 'tis true, 'tis true; and that is the glory of it. It is true. Come, worm, and prove it; come, pall; come, shroud; come, and prove it. Then come wings of faith, come, leap like a seraph; come, eternal ages, come, and ye shall prove that there are joys that the eye hath not seen, which the ear hath not heard, and which only God can reveal to us by his Spirit. Oh! my earnest prayer is that none of you may come short of this rest, but that ye may enter into it, and enjoy it for ever and ever. God give you his great blessing, for Jesus' sake! Amen.

3

No Tears
in Heaven[1]

And God shall wipe away all tears from their eyes.
Revelation 7:17

I t is an ill thing to be always mourning, sighing and complaining concerning the present. However dark it may be, we may surely recall some fond remembrances of the past. There were days of brightness, there were seasons of refreshing from the presence of the Lord. Be not slow to confess, O believing soul, that the Lord has been thy help! And though now thy burden be very heavy,

---

1.   This sermon was preached on Sunday morning, 6 August 1865, at the Metroplitan Tabernacle, Newington.

thou wilt find an addition to thy strength in the thought of seasons long since past, when the Lord lightened thy load, and made thy heart to leap for joy.

Yet more delightful will it be to expect the future. The night is dark, but the morning cometh. Over the hills of darkness the day breaketh. It may be that the road is rough, but its end is almost in view, Thou hast been clambering up the steep heights of Pisgah, and from the brow thereof thou mayest view thy glorious heritage. True the tomb is before thee, but thy Lord has snatched the sting from death, and the victory from the grave.

Do not, O burdened spirit, confine thyself to the narrow miseries of the present hour, but let thine eye gaze with fondness upon the enjoyment of the past, and view with equal ardour the infinite blessings of old eternity, when thou wast not, but when God set thee apart for himself, and wrote thy name in his book of life; and let thy glance flash forward to the future eternity, the mercies which shall be thine even here on earth, and the glories which are stored up for thee beyond the skies. I shall be well rewarded this morning if I shall minister comfort to one heavy spirit by leading it to remember the glory which is yet to be revealed.

Coming to our text, we shall observe, in the first place, that as God is to wipe away tears from the faces of the glorified, we may well infer that their eyes will be filled with tears till then; and in the second place, it is worthy of reflection that as God never changes, even now he is engaged in drying tears from his children's eyes; and then, coming right into the heart of the text, we shall dwell upon the great truth, that in heaven Divine Love removes all tears from the glorified; and so we shall close, by making some inquiry as to whether or not we belong to that happy company.

Our first subject of meditation is the inference *that tears are to fill the eyes of believers until they enter the promised rest.* There would be no need to wipe them away if there were none remaining. They come to the very gates of heaven weeping, and accompanied by their two comrades, sorrow and sighing; the tears are dried, and sorrow and sighing flee away. The weeping willow grows not by the river of the water of life, but it is plentiful enough below; nor shall we lose it till we change it for the palm-branch of victory. Sorrow's dewdrop will never cease to fall until it is transformed into the pearl of everlasting bliss.

> The path of sorrow, and that path alone,
> Leads to the place where sorrow is unknown.

Religion brings deliverance from the curse, but not exemption from trial.

The ancients were accustomed to use bottles in which to catch the tears of mourners, Methinks I see three bottles filled with the tears of believers. The first is *a common bottle*, the ordinary lachrymatory containing griefs incidental to all men, for believers suffer even as the rest of the race. *Physical pain* by no means spares the servants of God. Their nerves, and blood-vessels, and limbs, and inward organs, are as susceptible of disease as those of unregenerate men. Some of the choicest saints have lain longest on beds of sickness, and those who are dearest to the heart of God have felt the heaviest blows of the chastening rod. There are pains which, despite the efforts of patience, compel the tears to wet the cheeks. The human frame is capable of a fearful degree of agony, and few there be who have not at some time or other watered their couch with tears because of the acuteness of their pains.

Coupled with this, there are *the losses and crosses of daily life*. What Christian among you trades without occasional difficulties and serious losses? Have any of you a lot so easy that you have nothing to deplore? Are there no crosses at home? Are there no troubles abroad? Can you travel from the first of January to the last of December without feeling the weariness of the way? Have you no blighted field, no bad debt, no slandered name, no harsh word, no sick child, no suffering wife to bring before the Lord in weeping prayer? You must be an inhabitant of another planet if you have had no griefs, for man is born to trouble as the sparks fly upwards. No ship can navigate the Atlantic of earth without meeting with storms; it is only upon the Pacific of heaven that all is calm for evermore. Believers must through much tribulation, inherit the kingdom of heaven. 'Trials must and will befall.'

Death contributes to our woes; the heirs of immortality are often summoned to gather around the tomb. Who hath not lost a friend? If Jesus wept, expect not that we shall be without the tears of bereavement; the well-beloved Lazarus died, and so will our choicest friends. Parents will go before us, infants will be snatched from us, brothers and sisters will fall before the scythe of death. Impartial foe of all, thou sparest neither virtue nor vice, holiness nor sin; with equal foot thou treadest on the cherished loves of all!

The Christian knows also *disappointments* as bitter and as keen as other men. Judas betrays Christ, Ahithophel is a traitor to David. We have had our Ahithophels, and we may yet meet with our Judas. We have trusted in friends, and we have found their friendships fail. We have leaned upon what seemed a staff, and it has pierced us like a spear. You cannot, dear friends, traverse the wilderness of this world without discovering that thorns and thistles grow plenteously in it, and that, step as you may, your feet must sometimes feel their power to wound.

The sea of life is salt to all men. Clouds hover over every landscape. We may forget to laugh, but we shall always know how to weep. As the saturated fleece must drip, so must the human race, cursed by the Fall, weep out its frequent griefs.

I see before me *a second bottle*; it is *black and foul*, for it contains tears distilled by the force of the fires of sin. This bottle holds more than the first, and is far more regularly filled. Sin is more frequently the mother of sorrow than all the other ills of life put together. Dear brothers and sisters, I am convinced that we endure more sorrow from our sins than from God's darkest providence.

Mark our rebellions *want of resignation*! When a trouble comes it is not the trial which makes us groan so much as our rebellion against it. It is true the ox goad is thrust into us, but we kick against it, and then it hurts us far more. Like men with naked feet, we kick against the pricks. We head our vessel against the stream of God's will, and then murmur because the waves beat violently upon us. An unsubdued will is like a maniac's hand which tears himself. The chastisements which come directly from our heavenly Father are never so hard to bear as the frettings and fumings of our unhumbled self-will. As the bird dashes against the wires of its cage and breaks its own wing, even so do we. If we would take the cross as our gracious Father gives it, it would not gall our shoulders, but since we revolt from it and loathe the burden, our shoulders grow raw and sore, and the load becomes intolerable. More submission, and we should have fewer tears.

There are the tears, too, of *wounded, injured pride*, and how hot and scalding they are! When a man has been ambitious and has failed, how he will weep instead of standing corrected, or gathering up his courage for a wiser venture. When a friend has spoken slightingly of us, or an enemy has accused us, how we have had to put our fingers to our hot eyelids to keep the tears from streaming out, and have felt all the while as full of wretchedness as we well could be. Ah, these are cruel and wicked tears. God wipe them away from our eyes now! Certainly he must do it before we shall be able to enter heaven.

How numerous, too, are the tears of *unbelief*! We manufacture troubles for ourselves by anticipating future ills which may never come, or which, if they do come, may be like the clouds, all 'big with mercy', and 'break with blessings on our head'. We get supposing what we should do if such-and-such a thing occurred, which thing God has determined never shall occur. We imagine ourselves in positions where Providence never intends to place us, and so we feel a thousand trials in fearing one. That bottle, I say, ought never to carry within it a tear from a believer's eyes, and yet it has had whole floods poured into it. Oh, the wickedness of mistrust of God, and the bitterness with which that distrust is made to curse itself. Unbelief makes a rod for its own back; distrust of God is its own punishment; it brings such want of rest, such care, such tribulation of spirit into the mind, that he who loves himself and loves pleasure, had better seek to walk by faith and not by sight.

Nor must I forget the scalding drops of *anger against our fellow men*, and of petulance and irritation, because we cannot have our way with them; these are black and horrid damps, as noisome as the vaults of Tophet. May we ever be saved from such unholy tears!

Sometimes, too, there are streams which arise from *depressed spirits*, spirits desponding because we have neglected the means of grace and the God of grace. The consolations of God are small with us because we have been seldom in secret prayer; we have lived at a distance from the Most High, and we have fallen into a melancholy state of mind. I thank God that there shall never come another tear from our eyes into that bottle when eternal love shall take us up to dwell with Jesus in his kingdom.

We would never overlook *the third bottle*, which is the true crystal lachrymatory into which holy tears may drop, tears like the *lachrymæ Christi*, the tears of Jesus, so precious in the sight of God. Even these shall cease to flow in heaven. Tears of repentance, like glistening dewdrops fresh from the skies, are stored in this bottle; they are not of the earth, they come from heaven, and yet we cannot carry them thither with us. Good Rowland Hill used to say repentance was such a sweet companion that the only regret he could have in going to heaven, was in leaving repentance behind him, for he could not shed the tears of repentance there. Oh, to weep for sin! It is so sweet a sorrow that I would a constant weeper be! Like a dripping well, my soul would ever drop with grief that I have offended my loving, tender, gracious God.

Tears for *Christ's injured honour* and slightedness glisten in the crystal of our third bottle. When we hear Jesu's name blasphemed among men, or see his cause driven back in the day of battle, who will not weep then? Who can restrain his lamentations? Such tears are diamonds in Christ's esteem; blessed are the eyes which are mines of such royal treasure. If I cannot win crowns I will at least give tears. If I cannot make men love my Master, yet will I weep in secret places for the dishonour which they do him. These are holy drops, but they are all unknown in heaven.

Tears of *sympathy* are much esteemed by our Lord; when we 'weep with those that weep' we do well; these are never to be restrained this side the Jordan. Let them flow! the more of them the better for our spiritual health. Truly, when I think of the griefs of men, and above all, when I have communion with my Saviour in his suffering, I would cry with George Herbert:

> Come all ye floods, ye clouds, ye rains,
> Dwell in my eyes! My grief hath need
> Of all the watery things that nature can produce!
> Let every vein suck up a river to supply my eyes,
> My weary, weeping eyes, too dry for me,
> Unless they get new conduits, fresh supplies,
> And with my state agree.

It were well to go to the very uttermost of weeping if it were always of such a noble kind as fellowship with Jesus brings. Let us never cease from weeping over sinners as Jesus did over Jerusalem; let us endeavour to snatch the firebrand from the flame, and weep when we cannot accomplish our purpose.

These three receptacles of tears will always be more or less filled by us as long as we are here, but in heaven the first bottle will not be needed, for the wells of earth's grief will all be dried up, and we shall drink from living fountains of water unsalted by a tear; as for the second, we shall have no depravity in our hearts, and so the black fountain will no longer yield its nauseous stream; and as for the third, there shall be no place amongst celestial occupations for weeping even of the most holy kind.

Till then, we must expect to share in human griefs, and instead of praying against them, let us ask that they may be sanctified to us; I mean, of course, those of the former sort. Let us pray that tribulation may work patience, and patience experience, and experience the hope which maketh not ashamed. Let us pray that as the sharp edge of the graving tool is used upon us it may only remove our excrescencies and fashion us into images of our Lord and Master. Let us pray that the fire may consume nothing but the dross, and that the floods may wash away nothing but defilement. May we have to thank God that though before we were afflicted we went astray, yet now have we kept his word; and so shall we see it to be a blessed thing, a divinely wise thing, that we should tread the path of sorrow, and reach the gates of heaven with the teardrops glistening in our eyes.

Secondly, *even here if we would have our tears wiped away we cannot do better than return to our God.* He is the great tear wiper. Observe, brethren, that God can remove every vestige of grief from the hearts of his people by granting them complete resignation to his will. Our selfhood is the root of our sorrow. If self were perfectly conquered, it would be equal to us whether love ordained our pain or ease, appointed us wealth or poverty. If our will were completely God's will, then pain itself would be attended with pleasure, and sorrow would yield us joy for Christ's sake. As one fire puts out another, so the master passion of love to God and complete absorption in his sacred will quenches the fire of human grief and sorrow. Hearty resignation puts so much honey in the cup of gall that the wormwood is forgotten. As death is swallowed up in victory, so is tribulation swallowed up in complacency and delight in God.

He can also take away our tears by constraining our minds to dwell with delight upon the end which all our trials are working to produce. He can show us that they are working together for good, and as men of understanding, when we see that we shall be essentially enriched by our losses, we shall be content with them; when we see that the medicine is curing us of mortal sickness, and that our sharpest pains are only saving us from pains far more terrible, then shall we kiss the rod and sing in the midst of tribulation, 'Sweet affliction!' – sweet affliction, since it yields such peaceable fruits of righteousness.

Moreover, he can take every tear from our eye in the time of trial by shedding abroad the love of Jesus Christ in our hearts more plentifully. He can make it clear to us that Christ is afflicted in our affliction. He can indulge us with a delightful sense of the divine virtue which dwells in his sympathy, and make us rejoice to be co-sufferers with the angel of the covenant. The Saviour can make our hearts leap for joy by reassuring us that we are written on the palms of his hands, and that we shall be with him where he is. Sick beds become thrones, and hovels ripen into palaces when Jesus is made sure to our souls. My brethren, the love of Christ, like a great flood, rolls over the most rugged rocks of afflictions, so high above them that we may float in perfect peace where others are a total wreck. The rage of the storm is all hushed when Christ is in the vessel. The waters saw thee, O Christ, the waters saw thee and were silent at the presence of their king.

The Lord can also take away all present sorrow and grief from us by providentially removing its cause. Providence is full of sweet surprises and unexpected turns. When the sea has ebbed its uttermost, it turns again and covers all the sand. When we think the dungeon is fast, and that the bolt is rusted in, he can make the door fly open in a moment. When the river rolls deep and black before us, he can divide it with a word, or bridge it with his hand. How often have you found it so in the past? As a pilgrim to Canaan you have passed through the Red Sea, in which you once feared you would be drowned; the bitter wells of Marah were made sweet by God's presence; you fought the Amalekite, you went through the terrible wilderness, you passed by the place of the fiery serpents, and you have yet been kept alive, and so shall you be. As the clear shining cometh after rain, so shall peace succeed your trials. As fly the black clouds before the compelling power of the wind, so will the eternal God make your griefs to fly before the energy of his grace. The smoking furnace of trouble shall be followed by the bright lamp of consolation.

Still, the surest method of getting rid of present tears, is communion and fellowship with God, When I can creep under the wing of my dear God and nestle close to his bosom, let the world say what it will, and let the devil roar as he pleases, and let my sins accuse and threaten as they may, I am safe, content, happy, peaceful, rejoicing.

> Let earth against my soul engage,
> And hellish darts be hurled;
> Now I can smile at Satan's rage,
> And face a frowning world.

To say, 'My Father, God,' to put myself right into his hand, and feel that I am safe there; to look up to him, though it be with tears in my eyes, and feel that he loves me, and then to put my head right into his bosom as the prodigal did, and sob my griefs out there into my Father's heart, oh, this is the death of grief, and the life of all consolation. Is not Jehovah called the God of all comfort? You will find him so, beloved. He has been 'our help in ages past'; he is 'our hope for years to come'. If he had not been my help, then had my soul perished utterly in the day of its weariness and its heaviness, Oh, I bear testimony for him this day that you cannot go to him and pour out your heart before him without finding a delightful solace.

When your friend cannot wipe away the tear, when you yourself, with your strongest reasonings and your boldest efforts, cannot constrain yourself to resignation; when your heart beats high, and seems as if it would burst with grief, then ye people pour out your hearts before him. God is a refuge for us. He is our castle and high tower, our refuge and defence. Only go ye to him, and ye shall find that even here on earth God shall wipe away all tears from your eyes.

Now we shall have to turn our thoughts to what is the real teaching of the text, namely, *the removal of all tears from the blessed ones above.*

There are many reasons why glorified spirits cannot weep. These are well known to you, but let us just hint at them. *All outward causes of grief are gone.* They will never hear the toll of the knell in heaven. The mattock and the shroud are unknown things there. The horrid thought of death never flits across an immortal spirit. They are never parted; the great meeting has taken place to part no more. Up yonder they have no losses and crosses in business. 'They serve God day and night in his temple.' They know no broken friendships there. They have no ruined hearts, no blighted prospects. They know even as they are known, and they love even as they are loved. No pain can ever fall on them; as yet they have no bodies, but when their bodies shall be raised from the grave they shall be spiritualized so that they shall not be capable of grief. The tear-gland shall be plucked away; although much may be there that is human, at least the tear-gland shall be gone, they shall have no need of that organ; their bodies shall be unsusceptible of grief; they shall rejoice for ever. Poverty, famine, distress, nakedness, peril, persecution, slander, all these shall have ceased. 'The sun shall not light on them, nor any heat.' 'They shall hunger no more, neither thirst any more,' and therefore well may their tears cease to flow.

Again, *all inward evils will have been removed by the perfect sanctification wrought in them by the Holy Ghost.* No evil of heart, of unbelief in departing from the living God, shall vex them in paradise; no suggestions of the arch-enemy shall be met and assisted by the uprisings of iniquity within. They shall never be led to think hardly of God, for their hearts shall be all love; sin shall have no sweetness to them, for they shall be perfectly purified from all depraved desires. There shall be no lusts of the eye, no lusts of the flesh, no pride of life to be snares to their feet. Sin is shut out, and they are shut in. They are for ever blessed, because they are without fault before the throne of God. What a heaven must it be to be without spot, or wrinkle, or any such thing! Well may they cease to mourn who have ceased to sin.

All fear of change also has been for ever shut out. They know that they are eternally secure. Saints on earth are fearful of falling and some believers even dream of falling away; they think God will forsake them and that men will persecute and take them. No such fears can vex the blessed ones who view their Father's face. Countless cycles may revolve, but eternity shall not be exhausted; and while eternity endures, their immortality and blessedness shall co-exist with it. They dwell within a city which shall never be stormed, they bask in a sun which shall never set, they swim in a flood-tide which shall never ebb, they drink of a river which shall never dry, they pluck fruit from a tree which shall never be withered. Their blessedness knows not the thought, which would act like a canker at its heart, that it might, perhaps, pass away and cease to be. They cannot, therefore, weep, because they are infallibly secure, and certainly assured of their eternal blessedness.

Why should they weep, when every desire is gratified? They cannot wish for anything which they shall not have. Eye and ear, heart and hand, judgment, imagination, hope, desire, will, every faculty shall be satisfied. All their capacious powers can wish they shall continually enjoy. Though 'Eye hath not seen, nor ear heard the things which God hath prepared for them that love him,' yet we know enough, by the revelation of the Spirit, to understand that they are supremely blessed. The joy of Christ, which is an infinite fullness of delight, is in them. They bathe themselves in the bottomless, shoreless sea of Infinite Beatitude.

Still, dear friends, this does not quite account for the fact that all tears are wiped from their eyes. I like better the text which tells us that God shall do it, and I want you to think with me, of fountains of tears which exist even in heaven, so that the celestial ones must inevitably weep if God did not by a perpetual miracle take away their tears. It strikes me, that if God himself did not interfere by a perpetual outflow of abundant consolations, the glorified have very deep cause for weeping. You will say, 'How is this?'

Why, in the first place, if it were not for this, *what regrets they must have for their past sins.* The more holy a man is, the more he hates sin. It is a token of growth in sanctification, not that repentance becomes less acute, but that it becomes more and more deep. Surely, dear friends, when we shall be made perfectly holy, we shall have a greater hatred of sin. If on earth we could be perfectly holy, why, methinks we should do little else than mourn, to think that so foul, and black, and venomous a thing as sin had ever stained us; that we should offend against so good, so gracious, so tender, so abundantly loving a God. Why, the sight of Christ, 'the Lamb in the midst of the throne', would make them remember the sin from which he purged them; the sight of their heavenly Father's perfection would be blinding to them, if it were not that by some sacred means, which we know not, God wipes away all these tears from their eyes; and though they cannot but regret that they have sinned, yet perhaps they know that sin has been made to glorify God by the overcoming power of Almighty grace; that sin has been made to be a black foil, a sort of setting for the sparkling jewel of eternal, sovereign grace, and it may be that for this reason they shed no tears over their past lives. They sing, 'Unto him that hath loved us, and washed us from our sins in his blood'; but they sing that heavenly song without a tear in their eyes; I cannot understand how this may be, for I know I could not do so as I now am; let this be the best reason, that God has wiped away the tears from their eyes.

Again, do you not think, beloved, that the thought *of the vast expense of shame and woe which the Saviour lavished for their redemption must, in the natural order of things, be a constant source of grief?* We sing sometimes that hymn which reminds us of the angelic song before the throne, and in one of its verses the poet says:

> But when to Calvary they turn,
> Silent their harps abide;
> Suspended songs a moment mourn
> the God that loved and died.

Now, that is natural and poetical, but it is not true, for you know very well that there are no suspended songs in heaven, and that there is no mourning even over Christ 'that loved and died'. It seems to me, that if I were thoroughly spiritualized and in such a holy state as those are in heaven, I could not look at the Lamb without tears in my eyes. How could I think of those five Wounds; that bloody sweat in Gethsemane; that cruel crowning with the thorns in Gabbatha; that mockery and shame at Golgotha – how could I think of it without tears? How could I feel that he loved me and gave himself for me, without bursting into a passion of holy affection and sorrow? Tears seem to be the natural expression of such hallowed joy and grief –

> Love and grief my heart dividing,
> With my tears his feet I'll bathe.

I must think it would be so in heaven, if it were not that by a glorious method, I know not how, God shall wipe away even those tears from their eyes. Does it not need the interference of God to accomplish this wonder?

Is there not another cause for grief, namely, *wasted opportunities*? Beloved, when we once ascend to heaven, there will be no more feeding of Christ's hungry people; no giving drink to the thirsty; no visiting his sick ones, or his imprisoned ones; no clothing of the naked; there will be no instructing the ignorant; no holding forth the Word of God among 'a crooked and perverse generation'. It has been often and truly said, if there could be regrets in heaven, those regrets would be, that we have wasted so many opportunities of honouring Christ on earth, opportunities which will then be past for ever. Now in heaven their hearts are not steeled and hardened, so that they can look back upon sins of omission without sorrow. I believe there will be the tenderest form of conscience there, for perfect purity would not be consistent with any degree of hardness of heart. If they be sensitive and tender in heart, it is inevitable that they should look back with regret upon the failures of the life below unless some more mighty emotion should overwhelm that of contrition. I can say, beloved, if God would take me to heaven this morning, if he did not come in, and by a special act of his omnipotence, dry up that fountain of tears, I should almost forget the glories of paradise in the midst of my own shame, that I have not preached more earnestly, and have not prayed more fervently, and laboured more abundantly for Christ. That text, to which we heard a reference from a dear brother during the week, where Paul says, 'I call God to witness that for the space of three years I ceased not night and day with tears, to warn every one of you,' is a text that we cannot any of us read without blushes and tears; and in heaven, methinks, if I saw the Apostle Paul, I must burst out into weeping, if it were not for this text, which says that 'God shall wipe away *all* tears,' and these among them. Who but the Almighty God could do this!

Perhaps, again, another source of tears may suggest itself to you; namely, *regrets in heaven for our mistakes, and misrepresentations, and unkindnesses towards other Christian brethren.* How surprised we shall be to meet in heaven some whom we did not love on earth! We would not commune with them at the Lord's Table. We would not own that they were Christians. We looked at them very askance if we saw them in the street. We were jealous of all their operations. We suspected their zeal as being nothing better than rant, and we looked upon their best exertions as having sinister motives at the bottom. We said many hard things, and felt a great many more than we said. When we shall see these unknown and unrecognized brethren in heaven will not their presence naturally remind us of our offences against Christian love and spiritual unity?

I cannot suppose a perfect man, looking at another perfect man, without regretting that he ever ill-treated him: it seems to me to be the trait of a gentleman, a Christian, and of a perfectly sanctified man above all others, that he should regret having misunderstood, and misconstrued, and misrepresented one who was as dear to Christ as himself.

I am sure as I go round among the saints in heaven, I cannot (in the natural order of things) help feeling 'I did not assist you as I ought to have done. I did not sympathize with you as I ought to have done. I spoke a hard word to you. I was estranged from you.' And I think you would all have to feel the same; inevitably you must, if it were not that by some heavenly means, I know not how, the eternal God shall so overshadow believers with the abundant bliss of his own self that even that cause of tears shall be wiped away.

Has it never struck you, dear friends, that if you go to heaven and *see your dear children left behind unconverted*, it would naturally be a cause of sorrow? When my mother told me that if I perished she would have to say 'Amen' to my condemnation, I knew it was true and it sounded very terrible, and had a good effect on my mind; but at the same time I could not help thinking, 'Well, you will be very different from what you are now,' and I did not think she would be improved. I thought, 'Well, I love to think of your weeping over me far better than to think of you as a perfect being, with a tearless eye, looking on the damnation of your own child.'

It really is a very terrible spectacle, the thought of a perfect being looking down upon hell, for instance, as Abraham did, and yet feeling no sorrow; for you will recollect that, in the tones in which Abraham addressed the rich man, there is nothing of pity, there is not a single syllable which betokens any sympathy with him in his dreadful woes; and one does not quite comprehend that perfect beings, God-like beings, beings full of love, and everything that constitutes the glory of God's complete nature, should yet be unable to weep, even over hell itself; they cannot weep over their own children lost and ruined!

Now, how is this? If you will tell me, I shall be glad, for I cannot tell you. I do not believe that there will be one atom less tenderness, that there will be one fraction less of amiability, and love, and sympathy – I believe there will be more – but that they will be in some way so refined and purified, that while compassion for suffering is there, detestation of sin shall be there to balance it, and a state of complete equilibrium shall be attained. Perfect acquiescence in the divine will is probably the secret of it; but it is not my business to guess; I do not know what handkerchief the Lord will use, but I know that he will wipe all tears away from their faces, and these tears among them.

Yet, once again, it seems to me that spirits before the throne, taking, as they must do, a deep interest in everything which concerns the honour of the Lord Jesus Christ, must feel deeply grieved when they see the cause of truth imperilled, and the kingdom of Christ, for a time, put back.

Think of Luther, or Wycliffe, or John Knox, as they see the advances of Popery just now.

Take John Knox first, if you will. Think of him looking down and seeing cathedrals rising in Scotland, dedicated to the service of the Pope and the devil. Oh, how the stern old man, even in glory, methinks, would begin to shake himself; and the old lion lash his sides once more, and half-wish that he could come down and pull the nests to pieces that the rooks might fly away.

Think of Wycliffe looking down on this country where the gospel has been preached so many years and seeing monks in the Church of England, and seeing spring up in our national establishment everywhere, not disguised Popery as it was ten years ago, but stark naked Popery, downright Popery that unblushingly talks about the 'Catholic Church', and is not even Anglican any longer. What would Wycliffe say? Why, methink as he leans over the battlements of heaven, unless Wycliffe be mightily altered, and I cannot suppose he is (except for the better, and that would make him more tender-hearted and more zealous for God still), he must weep to think that England has gone back so far, and that on the dial of Ahaz the sun has beat a retreat.

I do not know how it is they do not weep in heaven, but they do not. The souls under the altar cry, 'How long? How long? How long?' There comes up a mighty intercession from those who were slaughtered in the days gone by for Christ: their prayer rises, 'How long? How long? How long?' and God as yet does not avenge his own elect though they cry day and night unto him. Yet that delay does not cost them a single tear. They feel so sure that the victory will come, they anticipate so much the more splendid a triumph because of its delay, and therefore they do both patiently hope and quietly wait to see the salvation of God. They know that without us they cannot be made perfect, and so they wait till we are taken up, that the whole company may be completed, and that then the soul may be dressed in its body, and they may be perfected in their bliss; they wait but they do not weep. They wait and they cry, but in their cry no sorrow has a place.

Now I do not understand this, because it seems to me that the more I long for the coming of Christ, the more I long to see his kingdom extended, the more I shall weep when things go wrong, when I see Christ blasphemed, his cross trampled in the mire, and the devil's kingdom established; but the reason is all in this, 'God shall wipe away all tears from their eyes.'

I thought I would just indicate to you why it says that God does it. It strikes me that these causes of tears could not be removed by an angel, could not be taken away by any form of spiritual enjoyment apart from the direct interposition of Almighty God. Think of all these things and wonder over them, and you will recall many other springs of grief which must have flowed freely if Omnipotence had not dried them up completely; then ask how it is that the saints do not weep and do not sorrow; and you cannot get any other answer than this – God has done it in a way unknown to us, for ever taking away from them the power to weep.

And now, beloved, Shall we be among this happy company? Here is the question, and the context enables us to answer it. 'They have washed their robes, and made them white in the blood of the Lamb.' There is their character. 'Therefore are they before the throne of God.' The blood is a sacred argument for their being there, the precious blood.

Observe, 'they washed their robes.' It was not merely their feet, their worst parts, but they washed their robes, their best parts. A man's robes are his most honoured attire; he puts them on, and he does not mind our seeing his robes. There may be filthiness beneath, but the robes are generally the cleanest of all. But you see they washed even them. Now it is the mark of a Christian that he not only goes to Christ to wash away his black sins, but to wash his duties too. I would not pray a prayer unwashed with Jesu's blood; I would not like a hymn I have sung to go up to heaven except it had first been bathed in blood; if I would desire to be clothed with zeal as with a cloak, yet I must wash the cloak in blood; though I would be sanctified by the Holy Spirit and wear imparted righteousness as a raiment of needlework, yet I must wash even that in blood.

What say you, dear friends? Have you washed in blood? The meaning of it is, have you trusted in the atoning sacrifice? 'Without shedding of blood there is no remission of sin.' Have you taken Christ to be your all in all? Are you now depending on him? If so, out of deep distress you shall yet ascend leaning on your Beloved to the throne of God, and to the bliss which awaiteth his chosen.

But if not, 'there is none other name,' there is no other way. Your damnation will be as just as it will be sure. Christ is 'the way', but if ye will not tread it ye shall not reach the end; Christ is 'the truth', but if you will not believe him, you shall not rejoice; Christ is 'the life', but if you will not receive him you shall abide among the dead, and be cast out among the corrupt. From such a doom may the Lord deliver us, and give us a simple confidence in the divine work of the Redeemer, and to him shall be the praise eternally. Amen.

4

Heavenly Worship[1]

And I looked and, lo, a Lamb stood on the Mount Sion, and with him an hundred forty and four thousand, having his Father's name written in their foreheads. And I heard a voice from heaven, as the voice of many waters, and as the voice of a great thunder: and I heard the voice of harpers harping with their harps; And they sung as it were a new song before the throne, and before the four beasts, and the elders; and no man could learn that song but the hundred and forty and four thousand, which were redeemed from the earth.
Revelation 14:1-3

The scene of this marvellous and magnificent vision is laid upon Mount Sion; by which we are to understand not Mount Sion upon earth, but Mount Sion which is above, 'Jerusalem, the mother of us all'. To the Hebrew mind, Mount Sion was a type of heaven, and very justly so. Among all the mountains of the earth none was to be found so famous as Sion. It was there

---

1.   A sermon preached on Sabbath morning, 28 December 1856, at the Music Hall, Royal Surrey Gardens.

that patriarch Abraham drew his knife to slay his son, it was there, too, in commemoration of that great triumph of faith, Solomon built a majestic temple, 'beautiful for situation and the joy of the whole earth'. That Mount Sion was the centre of all the devotions of the Jews.

> 'Up to her courts, with joys unknown,
> The sacred tribes repaired.'

Between the wings of the cherubim Jehovah dwelt; on the one altar there all the sacrifices were offered to high heaven. They loved Mount Sion, and often did they sing, when they drew nigh to her, in their annual pilgrimages, 'How amiable are thy tabernacles O Lord God of hosts, my King and my God!' Sion is now desolate; she hath been ravished by the enemy, she hath been utterly destroyed: her veil hath been rent asunder, and the virgin daughter of Sion is now siting in sackcloth and ashes, but, nevertheless, to the Jewish mind it must ever, in its ancient state, remain the best and sweetest type of heaven. John, therefore, when he saw this sight might have said, 'I looked, and, lo, a Lamb stood in heaven, and with him an hundred and forty and four thousand having his Father's name written in their foreheads: And I heard a voice from heaven, as the voice of many waters, and as the voice of a great thunder, and I heard the voice of harpers harping with their harps: And they sung as it were a new song before the throne, and before the four beasts, and the elders: and no man could learn that song but the hundred and forty and four thousand, which were redeemed from the earth.'

This morning I shall endeavour to show you, first of all, *the object of heavenly worship* – the Lamb in the midst of the throne; in the next place, we shall look at *the worshippers themselves*, and note their manner and their character; in the third place, we shall listen *to hear their song*, for we may almost hear it; it is like 'the noise of many waters and like great thunder'; and then we shall close by noting, that it is a new song which they sing, and by endeavouring to mention one or two reasons why it must necessarily be so.

1. In the first place, then, we wish to take a view of *The Object of Heavenly Worship*. The divine John was privileged to look within the gates of pearl; and on turning round to tell us what he saw – observe how he begins – he saith not, 'I saw streets of gold or walls of jasper,' he saith not, 'I saw crowns, marked their lustre and saw the wearers.' That he noticed afterwards. But he begins by saying, 'I looked, and, lo, a Lamb!' – to teach us that the very first and chief object of attraction in the heavenly state is 'the Lamb of God which taketh away the sins of the world'. Nothing else attracted the Apostle's attention so much as the person of that Divine Being, who is the Lord God, our most blessed Redeemer: 'I looked, and, lo, a Lamb!' Beloved, if we were allowed to look within the veil which parts us from the world of spirits, we should see, first of all, the person of our Lord Jesus. If now we could go where the immortal spirits 'day without night circle the throne rejoicing', we should see each of them with their faces turned in one direction; and if we should step up to one of the blessed spirits, and say, 'O bright immortal, why are thine eyes fixed? What is it that absorbs thee quite, and wraps thee up in vision?' He, without deigning to give an answer, would simply point to the centre of the sacred circle, and lo, we should see a Lamb in the midst of the throne. They have not yet ceased to admire his beauty, and marvel at his wonders and adore his person.

> 'Amidst a thousand harps and songs,
> Jesus, our God, exalted reigns.'

He is the theme of song and the subject of observation of all the glorified spirits and of all the angels in paradise. 'I looked, and, lo, a Lamb!'

Christian, here is joy for thee; thou hast looked, and thou hast seen the Lamb. Through tearful eyes thou hast seen the Lamb taking away thy sins. Rejoice, then. In a little while, when thine eyes shall have been wiped from tears, thou wilt see the same Lamb exalted on his throne. It is the joy of the heart to hold daily fellowship and communion with Jesus; thou shalt have the same joy in heaven. There shalt thou see him as he is, and thou shalt be like him. Thou shalt enjoy the constant vision of his presence, and thou shalt dwell with him for aye.

'I looked, and, lo, a Lamb!' Why, that Lamb is heaven itself, for as good Rutherford says, 'Heaven and Christ are the same things; to be with Christ is to be in heaven, and to be in heaven is to be with Christ.' And he very sweetly says in one of his letters, wrapped up in love to Christ: 'Oh! my Lord Christ, if I could be in heaven without thee, it would be a hell; and if I could be in hell, and have thee still, it would be a heaven to me, for thou art all the heaven I want.' It is true, is it not, Christian? Does not thy soul say so?

> 'Not all the harps above
> Could make a heavenly place,
> Should Christ his residence remove,
> Or but conceal his face.'

All thou needest to make thee blessed, supremely blessed, is 'to be with Christ, which is far better'.

And now observe *the figure under which Christ is represented in heaven.* 'I looked, and, lo, a Lamb.' Now, you know Jesus, in Scripture, is often represented as a lion; he is so to his enemies, for he devoureth them, and teareth them to pieces. 'Beware, ye that forget God, lest he tear you in pieces, and there be none to deliver.' But in heaven he is in the midst of his friends, and therefore he

> 'Looks like a lamb that has been slain,
> And wears his priesthood still.'

Why should Christ in heaven choose to appear under the figure of a lamb, and not in some other of his glorious characters? We reply, because it was as a lamb that Jesus fought and conquered, and therefore as a lamb he appears in heaven. I have read of certain military commanders, when they were conquerors, that on the anniversary of their victory they would never wear anything but the garment in which they fought. On that memorable day they say, 'Nay, take away the robes; I will wear the garment which has been embroidered with the sabre-cut, and garnished with the shot that hath riddled it; I will wear no other garb but that in which I fought and conquered.' It seems as if the same feeling possessed the breast of Christ. 'As a Lamb,' saith he, 'I died, and worsted hell; as a Lamb I have redeemed my people, and therefore as a Lamb I will appear in paradise.'

But, perhaps, there is another reason – it is to encourage us to come to him in prayer. Ah, believer, we need not be afraid to come to Christ, for he is a Lamb. To a lion-Christ we need fear to come: but the Lamb-Christ! – oh, little children, were ye ever afraid of lambs? Oh, children of the living God, should ye ever fail to tell your griefs and sorrows into the breast of one who is a Lamb? Ah, let us come boldly to the throne of the heavenly grace, seeing a Lamb sits upon it.

One of the things which tend very much to spoil our prayer-meetings is the fact that our brethren do not pray boldly. They would practise reverence, as truly they ought, but they should remember that the highest reverence is consistent with true familiarity. No man more reverent than Luther; no man more fully carried out the passage, 'He talked with his Maker as a man talketh with his friend.' We may be as reverent as the angels, and yet we may be as familiar as children in Christ Jesus. Now, our friends, when they pray, very frequently say the same thing every time. They are Dissenters; they cannot bear the Prayer Book; they think that forms of prayer are bad, but they always use their own form of prayer notwithstanding, as much as if they were to say that the bishop's form would not do, but their own they must always use. But a form of prayer being wrong is as much wrong when I make it as when the bishop makes it. I am as much out of order in using what I compose myself continually and constantly, as I am when I am using one that has been composed for me; perhaps far more so, as it is not likely to be one-half so good. If our friends, however, would lay aside the form into which they grow, and break up the stereotyped plates with which they print their prayers so often, they might come boldly to the throne of God, and need never fear to do so; for he whom they address is represented in heaven under the figure of a Lamb, to teach us to come close to him, and tell him all our wants, believing that he will not disdain to hear them.

And you will further notice that *this Lamb is said to stand*. Standing is the posture of triumph. The Father said to

Christ, 'Sit thou on my throne, till I make thine enemies thy footstool.' It is done, they are his footstool, and here he is said to stand erect, like a victor over all his enemies. Many a time the Saviour knelt in prayer; once he hung upon the cross; but when the great scene of our text shall be fully wrought out he shall stand erect, as more than conqueror, through his own majestic might. 'I looked, and, lo, a Lamb stood on the Mount Sion.' Oh, if we could rend the veil – if now we were privileged to see within it – there is no sight would so enthral us as the simple sight of the Lamb in the midst of the throne. My dear brethren and sisters in Christ Jesus, would it not be all the sight you would ever wish to see, if you could once believe him whom your soul loveth? Would it not be a heaven to you, if it were carried out in your experience – 'Mine eye shall see him, and not another's?' Would you want anything else to make you happy but continually to see him? Can you not say with the poet:

> 'Millions of years my wondering eyes
> Shall o'er my Saviour's beauty rove,
> And endless ages I'll adore
> The wonders of his love'?

And if a single glimpse of him on earth affords you profound delight, it must be, indeed, a very sea of bliss, and an abyss of paradise, without a bottom or a shore, to see him as he is – to be lost in his splendours, as the stars are lost in the sunlight, and to hold fellowship with him, as did John the beloved, when he leaned his head upon his bosom. And this shall be thy lot, to see the Lamb in the midst of the throne.

2. The second point is, *The Worshippers, Who are They?* Turn to the text, and you will note, first of all, *their numbers* – 'I looked, and, lo, a Lamb stood on the Mount Sion, and

with him an hundred forty and four thousand.' This is a certain number put for an uncertain – I mean uncertain to us, though not uncertain to God. It is a vast number, put for that 'multitude which no man can number', who shall stand before the throne of God.

Now, here is something not very pleasant to my friend Bigot yonder. Note the number of those who are to be saved. They are said to be a great number, even a 'hundred forty and four thousand', which is but a unit put for the vast innumerable multitude who are to be gathered home. Why, my friend, there are not so many as that belonging to your church. You believe that none will be saved but those who hear your minister, and believe your creed; I do not think you could find one hundred and forty-four thousand anywhere. You will have to enlarge your heart I think; you must take in a few more, and not be so inclined to shut out the Lord's people, because you cannot agree with them. I do abhor from my heart that continual whining of some men about their own little church as the 'remnant' – the 'few that are to be saved'. They are always dwelling upon strait gates and narrow ways, and upon what they conceive to be a truth, that but few shall enter heaven. Why, my friends, I believe there will be more in heaven than in hell. If you ask me why I think so, I answer, because Christ, in everything, is to 'have the pre-eminence', and I cannot conceive how he could have the pre-eminence if there are to be more in the dominions of Satan than in paradise. Moreover, it is said there is to be a multitude that no man can number in heaven; I have never read that there is to be a multitude that no man can number in hell.

But I rejoice to know that the souls of all infants, as soon as they die, speed their way to paradise. Think what a multitude there is of them! And then there are the just, and the redeemed of all nations and kindreds up till now; and there are better times coming, when the religion of Christ shall be universal; when he shall reign from pole to pole with illimitable sway; when kingdoms shall bow before him, and nations be born in a day; and in the thousand years of the great millennial state there will be enough saved to make up all the deficiencies of the thousands of years that have gone before. Christ shall have the pre-eminence at last; his train shall be far larger than that which shall attend the chariots of the grim monarch of hell. Christ shall be master everywhere, and his praise sounded in every land. One hundred and forty-four thousand were observed, the types and representatives of a far larger number who are ultimately to be saved.

But notice, whilst the number is very large, *how very certain it is*. By turning over the leaves of your Bible to a previous chapter of this book (Revelation 7), you will see that at the fourth verse it is written, that one hundred and forty-four thousand were sealed. And now we find there are one hundred and forty-four thousand saved; not 143,999, and 144,001, but exactly the number that are sealed. Now, my friends may not like what I am going to say; but if they do not like it, their quarrel is with God's Bible, not with me. There will be just as many in heaven as are sealed by God – just as many as Christ did purchase with his blood; all of them, and no more and no less. There will be just as many there as were quickened to life by the Holy Spirit, and were, 'born again, not of blood, nor of the will of the flesh, nor of the will of man, but of God'.

'Ah,' some say, 'there is that abominable doctrine of election.' Exactly so, if it be abominable; but you will never be able to cut it out of the Bible. You may hate it, and gnash and grind your teeth against it; but, remember, we can trace the pedigree of this doctrine, even apart from Scripture, to the time of the Apostles. Church of England ministers and members, you have no right to alter from me on the doctrine of election, if you are what you profess by your own Articles. You who love the old Puritans, you have no right to quarrel with me, for where will you find a Puritan who was not a strong Calvinist? You who love the fathers, you cannot differ from me. What say you of Augustine? Was he not, in his day, called a great and mighty teacher of grace? And I even turn to Roman Catholics, and, with all the errors of their system, I remind them that even in their body have been found those who have held that doctrine, and, though long persecuted for it, have never been expelled from the church. I refer to the Jansenists.

But, above all, I challenge every man who reads his Bible to say that that doctrine is not there. What saith the ninth of Romans? 'The children being not yet born, neither having done any good or evil, that the purpose of God according to election might stand, not of works, but of him that calleth; It was said unto her, The elder shall serve the younger.' And then it goes on to say to the carping objector – 'Nay, but, O man, who art thou that repliest against God? Shall the thing formed say to him that formed it, Why hast thou made me thus? Hath not the potter power over the clay, of the same lump to make one vessel unto honour, and another unto dishonour?' But enough on this subject.

One hundred and forty-four thousand, we say, is a certain number made to represent the certainty of the salvation of all God's elect, believing people. Now, some say that this doctrine has a tendency to discourage men from coming to

Christ. Well, you say so, but I have never seen it and, blessed be God, I have never proved it. So I have preached this doctrine ever since I began to preach, but I can say this – ye shall not (and I am now become a fool in glorying) ye shall not find among those who have not preached the doctrine, one who has been the instrument of turning more harlots, more drunkards and more sinners of every class from the error of their ways, than I have, by the simple preaching of the doctrine of free grace; and, while this has been so, I hold that no argument can be brought to prove that it has a tendency to discourage sinners, or bolster them up in sin. We hold, as the Bible says, that all the elect, and those only, shall be saved, but we hold that all who repent are elect, that all who believe are elect, and that all who go to Christ are elect. So that if any of you have in your heart a desire after heaven and after Christ; if you carry out that desire in sincere and earnest prayer, and are born again, you may as certainly conclude your election as you can conclude that you are alive. You must have been chosen of God before the foundation of the world, or you would never have done any of these things, seeing they are the fruits of election.

But why should it keep any one from going to Christ? 'Because', says one, 'if I go to Christ I may not be elect.' No, sir, if you go, you prove that you are elect. 'But', says another, 'I am afraid to go, in case I should not be elect.' Say as an old woman once said, 'If there were only three persons elected, I would try to be one of them and since he said, "He that believeth shall be saved," I would challenge God on his promise, and try if he would break it.' No, come to Christ; and if you do so, beyond a doubt you are God's elect from the foundation of the world, and therefore this grace has been given to you.

But why should it discourage you? Suppose there are a number of sick folk here, and a large hospital has been built. There is put up over the door, 'All persons who come shall be taken in.' At the same time it is known that there is a person inside the hospital who is so wise that he knows all who will come, and has written down the names of all who will come in a book, so that, when they come, those who open the doors will only say, 'How marvellously wise our Master was, to know the names of those who would come.' Is there anything dispiriting in that? You would go, and you would have all the more confidence in that man's wisdom, because he was able to know before that they were going.

'Ah, but', you say, 'it was ordained that some should come.' Well, to give you another illustration; suppose there is a rule that there always must be a thousand persons, or a very large number, in the hospital. You say, 'When I go perhaps they will take me in, and perhaps they will not.' 'But', says someone, 'there is a rule that there must be a thousand in: somehow or other they must make up that number of beds, and have that number of patients in the hospital.' You say, 'Then why should not I be among the thousand; and have not I the encouragement that whosoever goes shall not be cast out? And have I not again the encouragement, that if they will not go, they must be fetched in somehow or other; for the number must be made up, so it is determined and so it is decreed.' You would therefore have a double encouragement, instead of half a one, and you would go with confidence, and say, 'They must take me in, because they say they will take all in that come; and on the other hand, they must take me in, because they must have a certain number: that number is not made up, and why should not I be one?' Oh, never doubt about election. Believe in Christ, and then rejoice in election; do not fret about it till you have believed in Christ.

'I looked, and, lo, a Lamb stood on the Mount Sion, and with him an hundred and forty and four thousand.' And who were these people, 'having his Father's name written in their foreheads'? Not *Bs* for 'Baptists', not *Ws* for 'Wesleyans', not *Es* for 'Established Church'. They had their Father's name and nobody else's. What a deal of fuss is made on earth about our distinctions! We think such a deal about belonging to this denomination, and the other. Why, if you were to go to heaven's gates, and ask if they had any Baptists there, the angel would only look at you, and not answer you. If you were to ask if they had any Wesleyans, or members of the Established Church, he would say, 'Nothing of the sort.' But if you were to ask him whether they had any Christians there, 'Ay,' he would say, 'an abundance of them: they are all one now — all called by one name; the old brand has been obliterated, and now they have not the name of this man or the other, they have the name of God, even their Father, stamped on their brow.' Learn then, dear friends, whatever the connection to which you belong, to be charitable to your brethren, and kind to them, seeing that, after all, the name you now hold here will be forgotten in heaven, and only your Father's name will be there known.

One more remark here, and we will turn from the worshippers to listen to their song. It is said of all these worshippers that they learned the song before they went there. At the end of the third verse, it is said, 'No man could learn that song but the hundred and forty and four thousand, which were redeemed from the earth.' Brethren, we must begin heaven's song here below, or else we shall never sing it above. The choristers of heaven have all had rehearsals upon earth, before they sing in that orchestra. You think that, die when you may, you will go to heaven without being prepared. Nay, sir, heaven is a prepared place for a prepared people, and unless you are 'made meet to be partakers of the inheritance of the saints in light', you can never stand there among them. If you were in heaven without a new heart and a right spirit, you would be glad enough to get out of it, for heaven, unless a man is heavenly himself, would be worse than hell. A man who is unrenewed and unregenerate going to heaven would be miserable there. There would be a song – he could not join in it; there would be a constant hallelujah, but he would not know a note: and besides, he would be in the presence of the Almighty, even in the presence of the God he hates, and how could he be happy there? No sirs; ye must learn the song of paradise here, or else ye can never sing it. Ye must learn to sing –

> 'Jesus, I love thy charming name,
> 'tis music to my ears.'

You must learn to feel that 'sweeter sounds than music knows mingle in your Saviour's name', or else you can never chant the hallelujahs of the blest before the throne of the great 'I AM'. Take that thought, whatever else you forget; treasure it up in your memory, and ask grace of God that you may here be taught to sing the heavenly song, that afterwards in the land of the hereafter, in the home of the beatified, you may continually chant the high praises of him that loved you.

3. And now we come to the third and most interesting point, namely, *The Listening to Their Song*. 'I heard a voice from heaven, as the voice of many waters, and as the voice of a great thunder: and I heard the voice of harpers harping with their harps' singing – how loud and yet how sweet!

First, then, singing *how loud!* It is said to be like 'the voice of many waters'. Have you never heard the sea roar, and the fullness thereof? Have you never walked by the seaside, when the waves were singing, and when every little pebble stone did turn chorister, to make up music to the Lord God of hosts? And have you never in time of storm beheld the sea, with its hundred hands, clapping them in gladsome adoration of the Most High? Have you never heard the sea roar out his praise, when the winds were holding carnival – perhaps singing the dirge of mariners, wrecked far out on the stormy deep, but far more likely exalting God with their hoarse voice, and praising him who makes a thousand fleets sweep over them in safety and writes his furrows on their own youthful brow? Have you never heard the rumbling and booming of ocean on the shore, when it has been lashed into fury and has been driven upon the cliffs? If you have, you have a faint idea of the melody of heaven. It was 'as the voice of many waters'.

But do not suppose that it is the whole of the idea. It is not the voice of one ocean, but the voice of many, that is needed to give you an idea of the melodies of heaven. You are to suppose ocean piled upon ocean, sea upon sea – the Pacific piled upon the Atlantic, the Arctic upon that, the Antarctic higher still, and so ocean upon ocean, all lashed to fury, and all sounding with a mighty voice the praise of God. Such is the singing of heaven. Or if the illustration fails to strike, take another. We have mentioned here two or three times the mighty falls of Niagara. They can be heard at a tremendous distance, so awful is their sound. Now, suppose waterfalls dashing upon waterfalls, cataracts upon cataracts, Niagaras upon Niagaras, each of them sounding forth their mighty voices, and you have got some idea of the singing of paradise.

'I heard a voice like the voice of many waters.' Can you not hear it? Ah! if our ears were opened we might almost catch the song. I have thought sometimes that the voice of the Æolian harp, when it has swollen out grandly, was almost like an echo of the songs of those who sing before the throne; and on the summer eve, when the wind has come in gentle zephyrs through the forest, you might almost think it was the floating of some stray notes that had lost their way among the harps of heaven, and come down to us, to give us some faint foretaste of that song which hymns out in mighty peals before the throne of the Most High.

But why so loud? The answer is, because there are so many there to sing. Nothing is more grand than the singing of multitudes. Many have been the persons who have told me that they could but weep when they heard you sing in this assembly, so mighty seemed the sound when all the people sang 'Praise God from whom all blessings flow.' And, indeed, there is something very grand in the singing of multitudes. I remember hearing 12,000 sing on one occasion in the open air. Some of our friends were then present, when we concluded our service with that glorious hallelujah. Have you ever forgotten it? It was indeed a mighty sound; it seemed to make heaven itself ring again. Think, then, what must be the voice of those who stand on the boundless plains of heaven, and with all their might shout, 'Glory and honour and power and dominion unto him that sitteth on the throne, and to the Lamb for ever and ever.'

One reason, however, why the song is so loud is a very simple one, namely, because all those who are there think themselves bound to sing the fondest of all. You know our favourite hymn:

> 'Then loudest of the crowd I'll sing,
> While heav'n's resounding mansions ring
> With shouts of sov'reign grace.'

And every saint will join that sonnet, and each one lift up his heart to God, then how mighty must be the strain of praise that will rise up to the throne of the glorious God, our Father!

But note next, while it was a loud voice, how *sweet* it was. Noise is not music. There may be 'a voice like many waters', and yet no music. It was sweet as well as loud; for John says, 'I heard the voice of harpers harping with their harps.' Perhaps the sweetest of all instruments is the harp. There are others which give forth sounds more grand and noble, but the harp is the sweetest of all instruments. I have sometimes sat to hear a skilful harper, till I could say, 'I could sit and hear myself away,' whilst with skilful fingers he touched the chords gently, and brought forth strains of melody which flowed like liquid silver, or like sounding honey into one's soul. Sweet, sweet beyond sweetness; words can scarcely tell how sweet the melody. Such is the music of heaven. No jarring notes there, no discord, but all one glorious harmonious song. You will not be there, formalist, to spoil the tune; nor you, hypocrite, to mar the melody; there will be all those there whose hearts are right with God, and therefore the strain will be one great harmonious whole, without a discord. Truly do we sing –

'No groans to mingle with the songs
That warble from immortal tongues.'

And there will be no discord of any other sort to spoil the melody of those before the throne. Oh! my beloved hearers, that we might be there! Lift us up, ye cherubs! Stretch your wings, and bear us up where the sonnets fill the air. But if ye must not, let us wait our time.

'A few more rolling suns at most,
Will land us on fair Canaan's coast,'

and then we shall help to make the song, which now we can scarcely conceive, but which yet we desire to join.

4. We now close with a remark upon the last point: *Why is the Song said to be a New Song?* But one remark here. It will be a new song because the saints were never in such a position before as they will be when they sing this new song. They are in heaven now, but the scene of our text is something more than heaven. It refers to the time when all the chosen race shall meet around the throne, when the last battle shall have been fought, and the last warrior shall have gained his crown. It is not now that they are thus singing, but it is in the glorious time to come, when all the hundred and forty and four thousand – or rather, the number typified by that number – will be all safely housed and all secure. I can conceive the period. Time was – eternity now reigns. The voice of God exclaims, 'Are my beloved all safe?' The angel flies through paradise and returns with this message, 'Yea, they are.' 'Is Fearful safe? Is

Feeble-mind safe? Is Ready-to-halt safe? Is Despondency safe?' 'Yes, O King, they are,' says he. 'Shut-to the gates,' says the Almighty, 'they have been open night and day, shut them to now.' Then, when all of them shall be there, then will be the time when the shout shall be louder than many waters, and the song shall begin which will never end.

There is a story told in the history of brave Oliver Cromwell, which I use here to illustrate this new song. Cromwell and his Ironsides before they went to battle bowed the knee in prayer, and asked for God's help. Then, with their Bibles in their breasts, and their swords in their hands – a strange and unjustifiable mixture, but which their ignorance must excuse – they cried, 'The Lord of hosts is with us, the God of Jacob is our refuge'; and rushing to battle they sang –

> 'O Lord our God, arise and let,
> Thine enemies scattered be,
> And let all those that do thee hate
> Before thy presence flee.'

They had to fight uphill for a long time, but at last the enemy fled. The Ironsides were about to pursue them and win the booty, when the stern harsh voice of Cromwell was heard: 'Halt! Halt! Now the victory is won, before you rush to the spoil, return thanks to God.' And they sang some such song as this – 'Sing unto the Lord, for he has gotten us the victory! Sing unto the Lord.' It was said to have been one of the most majestic sights in that strange, yet good man's history. (I say that word without blushing, for good he was.) For a time the hills seemed to leap, whilst the vast multitude, turning from the slain, still stained with blood, lifted up their hearts to God. We say, again, it was a strange sight, yet a glad one.

But how great shall be that sight, when Christ shall be seen as a conqueror, and when all his warriors, fighting side by side with him, shall see the dragon beaten in pieces beneath their feet! Lo, their enemies are fled; they were driven like thin clouds before a Biscay gale. They are all gone – death is vanquished, Satan is cast into the lake of fire – and here stands the King himself, crowned with many crowns the victor of the victors. And in the moment of exaltation the Redeemer will say, 'Come let us sing unto the Lord.' And then, louder than the shout of many waters, they shall sing, 'Hallelujah! the Lord God Omnipotent reigneth!' And that will be the full carrying out of the great scene!

My feeble words cannot depict it. I send you away with this simple question, 'Shall *you* be there to see the conqueror crowned?' Have *you* 'a good hope through grace' that you shall? If so, be glad; if not, go to your houses, fall on your knees, and pray to God to save you from that terrible place which must certainly be your portion, instead of that great heaven of which I preach, unless you turn to God with full purpose of heart.

5

Glory[1]

Who hath called us unto his eternal glory.
1 Peter 5:10

A fortnight ago, when I was only able to creep to the front of this platform, I spoke to you concerning the future of our mortal bodies: 'We know that if our earthly house of this tabernacle were dissolved, we have a building of God, a house not made with hands, eternal in the heavens.' On the next Sabbath day we went a step further, and we did not preach so much about the

---

1. Delivered on Lord's-Day morning, 20 May 1883, at the Metropolitan Tabernacle, Newington.

resurrection of the body as upon the hope of glory for our entire nature, our text being, 'Christ in you, the hope of glory.' Thus, we have passed through the outer court, and have trodden the hallowed floor of the Holy Place, and now we are the more prepared to enter within the veil, and to gaze awhile upon the glory which awaits us. We shall say a little – and oh, how little it will be – upon that glory of which we have so sure a prospect, that glory which is prepared for us in Christ Jesus, and of which he is the hope! I pray that our eyes may be strengthened that we may see the heavenly light, and that our ears may be opened to hear sweet voices from the better land. As for me, I cannot say that I will speak of the glory, but I will try to stammer about it; for the best language to which a man can reach concerning glory must be a mere stammering. Paul did but see a little of it for a short time, and he confessed that he heard things that it was not lawful for a man to utter; and I doubt not that he felt utterly nonplussed as to describing what he had seen. Though a great master of language, yet for once he was overpowered; the grandeur of his theme made him silent. As for us, what can we do, where even Paul breaks down? Pray, dear friends that the Spirit of glory may rest upon you, that he may open your eyes to see as much as can at present be seen of the heritage of the saints.

We are told that 'eye hath not seen, nor ear heard, neither have entered into the heart of man, the things which God hath prepared for them that love him.' Yet the eye sees wonderful things. There are sunrises and sunsets, Alpine glories and ocean marvels which, once seen, cling to our memories throughout life; yet even when nature is at her best she cannot give us an idea of the supernatural glory which God has prepared for his people. The ear has heard sweet harmonies. Have we not enjoyed music which has thrilled us? Have we not listened to speech which has seemed to make our hearts dance within us? And yet no melody of harp, nor charm of oratory, can ever raise us to a conception of the glory which God hath laid up for them that love him. As for the heart of man, what strange things have entered it! Men have exhibited fair fictions, woven in the loom of fancy, which have made the eyes to sparkle with their beauty and brightness; imagination has revelled and rioted in its own fantastic creations, roaming among islands of silver and mountains of gold, or swimming in seas of wine and rivers of milk; but imagination has never been able to open the gate of pearl which shuts in the city of our God. No, it hath not yet entered the heart of man.

Yet the text goes on to say, 'but he hath revealed it unto us by his Spirit.' So that heaven is not an utterly unknown region, not altogether an inner brightness shut in with walls of impenetrable darkness. God hath revealed joys which he has prepared for his beloved; but mark you, even though they be revealed of the Spirit, yet it is no common unveiling, and the reason that it is made known at all is ascribed to the fact that 'the Spirit searcheth all things, yea, the deep things of God.' So we see that the glory which awaits the saints is ranked among the deep things of God, and he that would speak thereof after the manner of the oracles of God must have much heavenly teaching. It is easy to chatter according to human fancy, but if we would follow the sure teaching of the word of God we shall have need to be taught of the Holy Spirit, without whose anointing the deep things of God must be hidden from us.

Pray that we may be under that teaching while we dwell upon this theme. There are three questions which we will answer this morning. The first is, what is the destiny of the saints? – 'Eternal glory', says the text. Secondly, wherein doth this glory consist? I said we would answer the questions, but this is not to be answered this side the pearl gate. Thirdly, what should be the influence of this prospect upon our hearts? What manner of people ought we to be whose destiny is eternal glory? How should we live who are to live forever in the glory of the Most High?

1. First, *what, then is the Destiny of the Saints?* Our text tells us that God has 'called us unto his eternal glory'. 'Glory!' does not the very word astound you? 'Glory!' Surely that belongs to God alone! Yet the Scripture says 'glory', and glory it must mean, for it never exaggerates. Think of glory for us who have deserved eternal shame! Glory for us poor creatures who are often ashamed of ourselves! Yes, I look at my book again, and it actually says 'glory' – nothing less than glory. Therefore so must it be.

Now, since this seems so amazing and astonishing a thing, I would so speak with you that not a relic of incredulity may remain in your hearts concerning it. I would ask you to follow me while we look through the Bible, not quoting every passage, which speaks of glory, but mentioning a few of the leading ones.

This glory has been *promised*. What said David? In the seventy-third Psalm and twenty-fourth verse, we meet with these remarkable words: 'Thou shalt guide me with thy counsel, and afterward receive me to glory.' In the original Hebrew, there is a trace of David's recollection of Enoch's being translated; and, though the royal Psalmist did not expect to be caught away without dying, yet he did expect that after he had followed the guidance of the Lord here below, the great Father would stoop and raise up his child to be with himself for ever. He expected to be received into glory. Even in those dim days, when as yet the light of the gospel was but in its dawn, this prophet and king was able to say, 'Thou shalt afterward receive me to glory.'

Did he not mean the same thing when in the eighty-fourth Psalm, verse eleven, he said, 'The Lord will give grace and glory: no good thing will he withhold from them that walk uprightly'? Not only no good thing under the name of grace will God withhold from the upright, but no good thing under the head of glory. No good of heaven shall be kept from the saints; no reserve is even set upon the throne of the great King, for our Lord Jesus has graciously promised, 'To him that overcometh will I grant to sit with me in my throne, even as I also overcame, and am set down with my Father in his throne.' 'No good thing', not even amongst the infinitely good things of heaven, will God 'withhold from them that walk uprightly'.

If David had this persuasion, much more may we who walk in the light of the gospel. Since our Lord Jesus hath suffered and entered into his glory, and we know that we shall be with him where he is, we are confident that our rest shall be glorious.

Brethren, it is to this glory that we have been called. The people of God having been predestinated, have been called with an effectual calling – called so that they have obeyed the call, and have run after him who has drawn them. Now, our text says that he has 'called us unto his eternal glory by Christ Jesus'. We are called to repentance, we are called to faith, we are called to holiness, we are called to perseverance, and all this that we may afterwards attain unto glory. We have another Scripture of like import in 1 Thessalonians 2:12: 'Who hath called you unto his kingdom and glory.' We are called unto his kingdom according to our Lord's word, 'Fear not, little flock; for it is your Father's good pleasure to give you the kingdom.' We are called to be kings, called to wear a crown of life that fadeth not away, called to reign with Christ in his glory. If the Lord had not meant us to have the glory, he would not have called us unto it, for his calling is no mockery. He would not by his Spirit have fetched us out from the world and separated us unto himself if he had not intended to keep us from falling and preserve us eternally. Believer, you are called to glory; do not question the certainty of that to which God has called you.

And we are not only called to it, brethren, but glory is especially joined with justification. Let me quote Romans 8:30: 'Moreover whom he did predestinate, them he also called: and whom he called, them he also justified: and whom he justified, them he also glorified.' These various mercies are threaded together like pearls upon a string: there is no breaking the thread, no separating the precious things. They are put in their order by God himself, and they are kept there by his eternal and irreversible decree. If you are justified by the righteousness of Christ, you shall be glorified through Christ Jesus, for thus hath God purposed, and so must it be.

Do you not remember how salvation itself is linked with glory? Paul, in 2 Timothy 2:10, speaks of 'the salvation which is in Christ Jesus with eternal glory'. The two things are riveted together, and cannot be separated. The saved ones must partake of the glory of God; for this are they being prepared every day. Paul, in the ninth of Romans, where he speaks about the predestinating will of God, says in the twenty-third verse: 'The vessels of mercy, which he had afore prepared unto glory'. This is the process which commenced in regeneration and is going on in us every day in the work of sanctification. We cannot be glorified so long as sin remains in us; we must first be pardoned, renewed and sanctified, and then we are fitted to be glorified. By communion with our Lord Jesus we are made like to him, as saith the Apostle in 2 Corinthians 3:18: 'But we all, with open face beholding as in a glass the glory of the Lord, are changed into the same image from glory to glory, even as by the Spirit of the Lord.' It is very wonderful how by the wisdom of God everything is made to work this way.

Look at the blessed text in 2 Corinthians 4:17, where Paul says, 'For our light affliction, which is but for a moment, worketh for us a far more exceeding and eternal weight of glory'; where he represents that all that we can suffer, whether of body or of mind, is producing for us such a mass of glory that he is quite unable to describe it, and he uses hyperbolically language in saying, 'a far more exceeding and eternal weight of glory.' Oh, blessed men, whose very losses are their gains, whose sorrows produce their joys, whose griefs are big with heaven! Well may we be content to suffer if so it be that all things are working together for our good, and are helping to pile up the excess of our future glory.

Thus, then, it seems we are called to glory, and we are being prepared for it; is it not also a sweet thought that our present fellowship with Christ is the guarantee of it? In Romans 8:17 it is said, 'If so be that we suffer with him, that we may be also glorified together.' Going to prison with Christ will bring us into the palace with Christ; smarting with Christ will bring us into reigning with Christ; being ridiculed, and slandered, and despised for Christ's sake will bring us to be sharers of his honour, and glory, and immortality. Who would not be with Christ in his humiliation if this be the guarantee that we shall be with him in his glory? Remember those dear words of the Lord Jesus: 'Ye are they which have continued with me in my temptations. And I appoint unto you a kingdom, as my Father hath appointed unto me.' Let us shoulder the cross, for it leads to the crown. 'No cross, no crown': but he that has shared the battle shall partake in the victory.

I have not yet done, for there is a text, in Hebrews 2:10, which is well worthy of our consideration: we are to be brought to glory. It is said of our Lord that it 'became him, for whom are all things, in bringing many sons unto glory, to make the captain of their salvation perfect through sufferings.' See, beloved, we are called to glory, we are being prepared for it, and we shall be brought to it. We might despair of ever getting into the glory land if we had not One to bring us there, for the pilgrim's road is rough and beset with many foes; but there is a 'Captain of our salvation', a greater than Bunyan's Greatheart, who is conducting the pilgrim band through all the treacherous way, and he will bring the 'many sons' – where? – 'unto glory.' Nowhere short of that shall be their ultimatum. Glory, glory shall surely follow upon grace; for Christ the Lord, who has come into his glory, has entered into covenant engagements that he will bring all the 'many sons' to be with him.

Mark this, and then I will quote no more Scriptures: this glory will be for our entire manhood, for our body as well as for our soul. You know that text in the famous resurrection chapter in 1 Corinthians 15? Paul speaks of the body as being 'sown in dishonour', but he adds, 'it is raised in glory'; and then, in Philippians 3:21, he says of our divine Lord at his coming, 'Who shall change our vile body, that it may be fashioned like unto his glorious body, according to the working whereby he is able even to subdue all things unto himself.' What a wonderful change that will be for this frail, feeble, suffering body! In some respects it is not vile, for it is a wonderful product of divine skill, and power, and goodness; but inasmuch as it hampers our spiritual nature by its appetites and infirmities, it may be called a 'vile body'. It is an unhandy body for a spirit: it fits a soul well enough, but a spirit wants something more ethereal, less earth-bound, more full of life than this poor flesh and blood and bone can ever be. Well, the body is to be changed. What alteration will it undergo? It will be rendered perfect. The body of a child will be fully developed, and the dwarf will attain to full stature. The blind shall not be sightless in heaven, neither shall the lame be halt, nor shall the palsied tremble. The deaf shall hear, and the dumb shall sing God's praises. We shall carry none of our deficiencies or infirmities to heaven. As good Mr Ready-to-halt did not carry his crutches there, neither shall any of us need a staff to lean upon. There we shall not know an aching brow, or a weak knee, or a failing eye. 'The inhabitant shall no more say, I am sick.'

And it shall be an impassive body, a body that will be incapable of any kind of suffering: no palpitating heart, no sinking spirit, no aching limbs, no lethargic soul shall worry us there. No, we shall be perfectly delivered from every evil of that kind. Moreover, it shall be an immortal body. Our risen bodies shall not be capable of decay, much less of death. There are no graves in glory. Blessed are the dead that die in the Lord, for their bodies shall rise, never to know death and corruption a second time. No smell or taint of corruption shall remain upon those whom Jesus shall call from the tomb. The risen body shall be greatly increased in power: it is 'sown in weakness', says the Scripture, but it is 'raised in power'. I suppose there will be a wonderful agility about our renovated frame: probably it will be able to move as swiftly as the lightning flash, for so do angels pass from place to place, and we shall in this, as in many things else, be as the angels of God. Anyhow, it will be a 'glorious body', and it will be 'raised in glory', so that the whole of our manhood shall participate of that wonderful depth of bliss which is summed up in the word 'glory'. Thus, I think I have set before you much of what the word of God saith upon this matter.

2. Secondly, may the Holy Spirit help me while I try very hesitatingly and stammeringly to answer the enquiry, *Wherein doth this Destiny consist?* Do you know how much I expect to do? It will be but little. You remember what the Lord did for Moses when the man of God prayed, 'I beseech thee, show me thy glory!' All that the Lord himself did for Moses was to say, 'Thou shalt see my back parts; but my face shall not be seen.' How little, then, can we hope to speak of this glory! Its back parts are too bright for us: as for the face of that glory, it shall not be seen by any of us here below, though by and by we shall behold it. I suppose if one who had been in glory could come straight down from heaven, and occupy this platform, he would find that his discoveries could not be communicated because of the insufficiency of language to express such a weight of meaning.

The saints' destiny is glory. What is glory, brethren? What is it, I mean, among the sons of men? It is generally understood to be fame, a great repute, the sound of trumpets, the noise of applause, the sweets of approbation among the crowd and in high places. The Queen of Sheba came from afar to see the glory of Solomon. What was that glory, brethren? It was the glory of a rare wisdom excelling all others: it was the glory of immense riches expended upon all manner of magnificence and splendour. As for this last glory, the Lord says of it that a lily of the field had more of it than Solomon; at least, 'Solomon in all his glory was not arrayed like one of these.' Yet that is what men mean by glory – rank, position, power, conquest – things that make the ears of men to tingle when they hear of them – things extraordinary and rare. All this is but a dim shadow of what God means by glory; yet out of the shadow we may obtain a little inkling of what the substance must be. God's people shall be wise, and even famous, for they shall 'shine as the stars for ever and ever'. God's people shall be rich; the very streets of their abode are paved with gold exceeding rich and rare. God's people shall be singularly honoured; there shall be a glory about them unrivalled, for they shall be known as a peculiar people, a royal priesthood, a race of beings lifted up to reveal their Maker's character beyond all the rest of his works.

I reckon that glory to a saint means, first of all, purified character. The brightest glory that really can come to anyone is the glory of character. Thus God's glory among men is his goodness, his mercy, his justice, his truth. But shall such poor creatures as we are ever have perfect characters? Yes, we shall one day be perfectly holy. God's Holy Spirit, when he has finished his work, will leave in us no trace of sin: no temptation shall be able to touch us; there will be in us no relics of our past and fallen state. Oh, will not that be blessed? I was going to say it is all the glory I want – the glory of being perfect in character, never sinning, never judging unjustly, never thinking a vain thought, never wandering away from the perfect law of God, never vexed again with sin which has so long been my worst enemy. One day we shall be glorious because the devil himself will not be able to detect a fault in us, and those eyes of God which burn like fire and read the inmost secrets of the soul, will not be able to detect anything blameworthy in us. Such shall be the character of the saints that they shall be meet to consort with Christ himself, fit company for that thrice Holy Being before whom angels veil their faces. This is glory!

Next, I understand by 'glory' our perfected manhood. When God made Adam, he was a far superior being to any of us. Man's place in creation was very remarkable. The Psalmist says, 'For thou hast made him a little lower than the angels, and hast crowned him with glory and honour. Thou madest him to have dominion over the works of thy hands; thou hast put all things under his feet: all sheep and oxen, yea, and the beasts of the field; the fowl of the air, and the fish of the sea, and whatsoever passeth through the paths of the seas.' No king among men in these days could rival Adam in the Garden of Eden: he was indeed monarch of all that he surveyed, and from the lordly lion down to the tiniest insect of all, living creatures paid him willing homage. Can we ever rise to this last honour? Brethren, listen, 'It doth not yet appear what we shall be, but we know that when Christ shall appear we shall be like him, for we shall see him as he is.' Is there any limit to the growth of the mind of a man? Can we tell what he may reach? We read of Solomon that God gave him largeness of heart as the sand of the sea: God will give to his people glory that will include in it more largeness of heart than Solomon ever knew. Then shall we know even as we are known by God. Now we see, but it is 'through a glass darkly', but then we shall see 'face to face'. You have met with men of great intellect and you have looked imp to them: but assuredly the smallest babe in Christ when he shall reach heaven shall have a greater intellect than the most profound philosopher who has ever astounded mankind by his discoveries. We shall not always be as we are today, contracted and hampered because of our little knowledge, and our slender faculties, and our dull perceptions. Our ignorance and prejudice shall vanish. What a man will become we can scarcely tell when he is remade in the image of God, and made like unto our divine Lord who is 'the firstborn among many brethren'. Here we are but in embryo: our minds are but the seeds, or the bulbs, out of which shall come the flower and glory of a nobler manhood. Your body is to be developed into something infinitely brighter and better than the bodies of men here below: and as for the soul, we cannot guess to what an elevation it shall be raised in Christ Jesus. There is room for the largest expectation here, as we conjecture what will be the full accomplishment of the vast intent of eternal love, an intent which has involved the sacrifice of the only begotten Son of God. That can be no mean design which has been carried on at the expense of the best that heaven itself possessed.

Further, by 'glory' and coming to glory I think we must understand complete victory. Dwelling in the age of the Romans, men said to themselves, as they read the Scriptures, 'What does the Apostle mean by "glory"?' and they could scarcely help connecting it with conquest, and the return of the warrior in triumph. Men called it glory in those days when valiant warriors returned from fields of blood with captives and spoil. Then did the heroes ride through the streets of Rome, enjoying a triumph voted them by the senate. Then for the while the men of war were covered with glory, and all the city was glorious because of them. As Christians, we hate the word 'glory' when it is linked with wholesale murder, and girt in garments rolled in blood; but yet there is a kind of fighting to which you and I are called, for we are soldiers of the cross; and if we fight valiantly under our great Captain, and rout every sin, and are found faithful even unto death, then we shall enter glory, and receive the honour which belongs to men who have fought a good fight, and have kept the faith. It will be no small glory to obtain the crown of life, which fadeth not away. Is not this a full glory if we only place these three things together: a purified character, a perfected nature and a complete victory?

An invaluable ingredient in true glory is the divine approval. 'Glory' among men means approbation: it is a man's glory when he is honoured of his Queen, and she hangs a medal on his breast, or when his name is mentioned in the high court of Parliament, and he is ennobled for what he has done. If men speak of our actions with approval, it is called fame and glory. Oh, but one drop of the approbation of God has more glory in it than a sea full of human praise; and the Lord will reward his own with this holy favour. He will say, 'Well done, good and faithful servant,' and Christ before the universe will say, 'Come, ye blessed of my Father.' Oh, what glory that will be! They were despised and rejected of men; they 'wandered about in sheepskins and goatskins; destitute, afflicted, tormented'; but now God approves them, and they take seats among the peers of heaven, made noble by the approbation of the Judge of all. This is glory with an emphasis, substantial glory. One approving glance from the eye of Jesus, one accepting word from the mouth of the Father, will be glory enough for any one of us, and this we shall have if we follow the Lamb whithersoever he goeth.

But this is not all: children of God will have the glory of reflecting the glory of God. When any of God's unfallen creatures shall wish to see the greatness of God's goodness, and mercy, and love, they that dwell in heaven will point out a glorified saint. Whenever any spirit from far-off regions desires to know what is meant by faithfulness and grace, some angel will reply, 'Go and talk with those who have been redeemed from among men.' I believe that you and I will spend much of eternity in making known to principalities and powers the unsearchable riches of the grace of God. We shall be mirrors reflecting God; and in us shall his glory be revealed. There may be myriads of races of pure and holy beings of whom we have never heard as yet, and these may come to the New Jerusalem as to the great metropolis of Jehovah's universe, and when they come there they will gaze upon the saints as the highest instances of divine grace, wisdom, power and love. It will be their highest pleasure to hear how eternal mercy dealt with us unworthy ones. How we shall delight to rehearse to them the fact of the Father's eternal purpose, the story of the incarnate God – the God that loved and died, and the love of the blessed Spirit who sought us in the days of our sin, and brought us to the cross-foot, renewing us in the spirit of our minds, and making us to be sons of God. Oh, brothers and sisters, this shall be our glory, that God shall shine through us to the astonishment of all.

Yet I think glory includes somewhat more than this. In certain cases, a man's glory lies in his relationships. If any of the royal family should come to your houses, you would receive them with respect; yes, and even as they went along the street they would be spied out, and passers-by would say, 'That is the prince!' and they would honour the son of our good Queen. But royal descent is a poor business compared with being allied to the King of kings. Many angels are exceeding bright, but they are only servants to wait upon the sons. I believe that there will be a kind of awe upon the angels at the sight of men; when they see us in our glory they will rejoice to know our near relation to their Lord, and to fulfil their own destiny as ministering spirits appointed to minister to the heirs of salvation. No pride will be possible to the perfected, but we shall then realize the exalted position to which, by our new birth and the divine adoption, we have been raised. 'Behold what manner of love the Father hath bestowed upon us, that we should be called the sons of God.' Sons of God! Sons of the Lord God Almighty! Oh what glory this will be!

Then there will be connected with this the fact that we shall be connected with Jesus in everything. For do not you see, brethren, it was because of our fall that Christ came here to save men; when he wrought out a perfect righteousness, it was all for us; when he died, it was all for us; and when he rose again, it was all for us? And what is more, we lived in Christ, we died in him, we were buried in him and rose in him, and we shall ascend into heaven to reign with him. All our glory is by Christ Jesus and in all the glory of Christ Jesus we have a share. We are members of his body; we are one with him. I say, the creatures that God has made, when they shall come to worship in the New Jerusalem, will stand and gaze at glorified men, and with bated breath will say one to another, 'These are the beings whose nature the Son of God assumed! These are the chosen creatures whom the Prince of heaven bought with his own blood.' They will stand astonished at the divine glory which will be manifested in beings emancipated from sin and hell and made heirs of God, joint-heirs with Jesus Christ. Will not even angels be surprised and awed as they look on the Church and say to one another, 'This is the bride, the Lamb's wife!' They will marvel how the Lord of glory should come to this poor earth to seek a spouse and that he should enter into eternal union with such a people. Glory, glory dwelleth in Immanuel's land! Now we are getting near to the centre of it. I feel inclined, like Moses, to put off my shoes from off my feet, for the place whereon we stand is holy ground, now that we are getting to see poor bushes like ourselves aglow with the indwelling God, and changed from glory unto glory.

And yet this is not all, for there in heaven we shall dwell in the immediate presence of God. We shall dwell with him in nearest and dearest fellowship! All the felicity of the Most High will be our felicity. The blessedness of the triune Jehovah shall be our blessedness for ever and ever. Did you notice that our text says, 'He hath called us unto his glory'? This outshines everything: the glory which the saints will have is the same glory which God possesses, and such as he alone can bestow. Listen to this text: 'Whom he justified, them he also glorified.' He glorifies them, then! I know what it is to glorify God, and so do you, but when we poor creatures glorify God it is in a poor way, for we cannot add anything to him. But what must it be for God himself to glorify a man! The glory, which you are to have for ever, my dear believing brother, is a glory which God himself will put upon you. Peter, as a Hebrew, perhaps uses a Hebraism when he says 'his glory': it may be that he means the best of glory that can be, even as the Jews were wont to say 'The trees of God' when they meant the greatest trees, or 'the mountains of God' when they intended the highest mountains; so by the glory of God Peter may mean the richest, fullest glory that can be. In the original, the word 'glory' has about it the idea of 'weight', at which the apostle Paul hints when he speaks of a 'weight of glory'. This is the only glory that has weight in it, all else is light as a feather. Take all the glories of this world, and they are outweighed by the small dust of the balance. Place them here in the hollow of my hand, all of them: a child may blow them away as thistledown. God's glory has weight; it is solid, true, real, and he that gets it possesses no mere name, or dream, or tinsel, but he has that which will abide the rust of ages and the fire of judgment.

The glory of God! How shall I describe it! I must set before you a strange Scriptural picture. Mordecai must be made glorious for his fidelity to his king, and singular is the honour which his monarch ordains for him. This was the royal order: 'Let the royal apparel be brought which the king useth to wear, and the horse that the king rideth upon, and the crown royal which is set upon his head: and let this apparel and horse be delivered to the hand of one of the king's most noble princes, that they may array the man withal whom the king delighteth to honour, and bring him on horseback through the street of the city, and proclaim before him, Thus shall it be done to the man whom the king delighteth to honour.' Can you not imagine the surprise of the Jew when robe and ring were put upon him, and when he found himself placed upon the king's horse. This may serve as a figure of that which will happen to us: we shall be glorified with the glory of God. The best robe, the best of heaven's array, shall be appointed unto us, and we shall dwell in the house of the Lord forever.

Highest of all our glory will be the enjoyment of God himself. He will be our exceeding joy: this bliss will swallow up every other, the blessedness of God. 'The Lord is my portion, saith my soul.' 'Whom have I in heaven but thee? and there is none upon earth that I desire beside thee.' Our God shall be our glory.

Yet bear with me, I have left out a word again: the text has it, 'Unto his eternal glory.' Ay, but that is the gem of the ring. The glory, which God has in reserve for his chosen will never come to an end: it will stay with us, and we shall stay with it, forever. It will always be glory, too; its brightness will never become dim; we shall never be tired of it, or sated with it. After ten thousand thousand millions of years in heaven, our happiness shall be as fresh as when it first began. Those are no fading laurels, which surround immortal brows. Eternal glory knows no diminution. Can you imagine a man being born at the same time that Adam was created and living all these thousands of years as a king like Solomon, having all he could desire? His would seem to be a glorious life. But, if at the end of seven thousand years that man must needs die, what has it profited him? His glory is all over now: its fires have died out in ashes. But you and I, when we once enter glory, shall receive what we can neither lose nor leave. Eternity! Eternity! This is the sweetness of all our future bliss. Rejoice, ye saintly ones! Take your harps down from the willows, any of you who are mourning and if you never sang before, yet sing this morning, 'God has called us unto his eternal glory,' and this is to be our portion world without end.

3. I can only find time for a few words upon the concluding head, which is – *What influence should all this have upon our hearts?* I think, first, it ought to excite desire in many here present that they might attain unto glory by Christ Jesus. Satan, when he took our blessed Lord to the top of an exceeding high mountain, tempted him to worship him by offering him the kingdoms of the world and all the glories thereof. Satan is very clever, and I will at this time take a leaf out of his book. Will you not fall down and worship the Lord Jesus when he can give you the kingdom of God and all the glory thereof, and all this, not in pretence, but in reality? If there was any force in the temptation to worship Satan for the sake of the glory of this world, how much more reason is there for urging you to worship the Son of God that you may obtain his salvation with eternal glory! I pray the Holy Ghost to drop a hot desire into many a poor sinner's breast this morning that he may cry, 'If this glory is to be had, I will have it, and I will have it in God's way, for I will believe in Jesus, I will repent, I will come to God, and so obtain his promise.'

Secondly, this ought to move us to the feeling of fear. If there be such a glory as this, let us tremble lest by any means we should come short of it. Oh, my dear hearers, especially you that are my fellow members, brother church officers, and workers associated with me, what a dreadful thing it will be if any one of us should come short of this glory! Oh, if there were no hell, it would be hell enough to miss of heaven! What if there were no pit that is bottomless, nor worm undying, nor fire unquenchable, it would be boundless misery to have a shadow of a fear of not reaching to God's eternal glory! Let us there pass the time of our sojourning here in fear, and let us watch unto prayer and strive to enter in at the strait gate. God grant we may be found of him at last to praise and honour!

If we are right, how this ought to move us to gratitude. Think of this, we are to enjoy 'his eternal glory'! What a contrast to our deserts! Shame and everlasting contempt are our righteous due apart from Christ. If we were to receive according to our merits, we should be driven from his presence and from the glory of his power. Verily, he hath not dealt with us after our sins, nor rewarded us according to our iniquities; for, after all our transgressions, he has still reserved us for glory, and reserved glory for us. What love and zeal should burn in our bosoms because of this!

Last of all, it should move us to a dauntless courage. If this glory is to be had, do we not feel like the heroes in Bunyan's picture? Before the dreamer there stood a fair palace, and he saw persons walking upon the top of it, clad in light, and singing. Around the door stood armed men to keep back those who would enter. Then a brave man came up to one who had a writer's inkhorn by his side, and said. 'Set down my name'; and straightway the warrior drew his sword, and fought with all his might, until he had cut his way to the door, and then he entered, and they within were heard to sing, 'Come in, come in, Eternal glory thou shalt win.'

Will you not draw your swords this morning, and fight against sin, till you have overcome it? Do you not desire to win Christ, and to be found in him? Oh, let us now begin to feel a passion for eternal glory, and then in the strength of the Spirit, and in the name of Jesus, let us press forward till we reach it. Even on earth we may taste enough of this glory to fill us with delight. The glory which I have described to you dawns on earth though it only comes to its noontide in heaven: the glory of sanctified character, the glory of victory over sin, the glory of relationship to God, the glory of union with Christ – these are all to be tasted in a measure here below. These glories send their beams down even to these valleys and lowlands. Oh, to enjoy them today and thus to have earnests and foretastes of glory. If we have them, let us go singing on until we reach the place where God's eternal glory shall surround us. Amen.

6

The Beatific Vision[1]

We shall see him as he is.
1 John 3:2

It is one of the most natural desires in all the world, that when we hear of a great and a good man, we should wish to see his person. When we read the works of any eminent author, we are accustomed to turn to the frontispiece to look for his portrait. When we hear of any wondrous deed of daring, we will crowd our windows to see the warrior ride through the streets. When we know of

---

1. A sermon delivered on Sabbath morning, 20 January 1856, at New Park Street Chapel, Southwark.

any man who is holy and who is eminently devoted to his work, we will not mind tarrying anywhere, if we may but have a glimpse of him whom God has so highly blessed. This feeling becomes doubly powerful when we have any connection with the man; when we feel not only that he is great, but that he is great for us; not simply that he is good, but that he is good to us; not only that he is benevolent, but that he has been a benefactor to us as individuals. Then the wish to see him rises to a craving desire, and the desire is insatiable until it can satisfy itself in seeing that unknown, and hitherto unseen donor, who has done such wondrously good deeds for us.

I am sure, my brethren, you will all confess that this strong desire has arisen in your minds concerning the Lord Jesus Christ. We owe to none so much; we talk of none so much, we hope, and we think of none so much: at any rate, no one so constantly thinks of us. We have I believe, all of us who love his name, a most insatiable wish to behold his person. The thing for which I would pray above all others, would be for ever to behold his face, for ever to lay my head upon his breast, for ever to know that I am his, for ever to dwell with him. Ay, one short glimpse, one transitory vision of his glory, one brief glance at his marred, but now exalted and beaming countenance, would repay almost a world of trouble.

We have a strong desire to see him. Nor do I think that that desire is wrong. Moses himself asked that he might see God. Had it been a wrong wish arising out of vain curiosity, it would not have been granted, but God granted Moses his desire: he put him in the cleft of the rock, shaded him with his hands, bade him look at the skirts of his garments, because his face could not be seen. Yea, more;

the earnest desire of the very best of men has been in the same direction. Job said, 'I know that my Redeemer liveth, and though worms devour this body, yet in my flesh shall I see God'; that was his desire. The holy Psalmist said, 'I shall be satisfied when I awake with thy likeness'; 'I shall behold thy face in righteousness.' And most saints on their deathbeds have expressed their fondest, dearest, and most blessed wish for heaven, in the expression of longing; 'to be with Christ, which is far better.' And not ill did our sweet singer of Israel put the words together, when he humbly said, and sweetly too:

> Millions of years my wondering eyes
> Shall o'er thy beauties rove;
> And endless ages I'll adore
> The glories of thy love.

We are rejoiced to find such a verse as this, for it tells us that our curiosity shall be satisfied, our desire consummated, our bliss perfected. 'We shall see him as he is.' Heaven shall be ours, and all we ever dreamed of him shall be more than in our possession.

By the help of God's mighty Spirit, who alone can put words in our mouths, let us speak first of all concerning *the glorious position* – 'As He is'; secondly, *his personal identity* – 'We shall see HIM as *he is*'; thirdly, *the positive vision* – 'we SHALL SEE him as he is'; and fourthly, *the actual persons* – 'WE shall see him as he is.'

First then, *The Glorious Position*. Our minds often revert to Christ as he was, and as such we have desired to see him. Ah! how often have we wished to see the babe that slept in Bethlehem! How earnestly have we desired to see the man who talked with the woman at the well! How frequently have we wished that we might see the blessed Physician walking amongst the sick and dying, giving life with his touch, and healing with his breath! How frequently too have our thoughts retired to Gethsemane, and we have wished our eyes were strong enough to pierce through eighteen hundred and fifty years which part us from that wondrous spectacle, that we might see him as he was!

We shall never see him thus; Bethlehem's glories are gone for ever; Calvary's glooms are swept away; Gethsemane's scene is dissolved; and even Tabor's splendours are quenched in the past. They are as things that were; nor shall they ever have a resurrection. The thorny crown, the spear, the sponge, the nails – these are not. The manger and the rocky tomb are gone. The places are there, unsanctified by Christian feet, unblessed, unhallowed by the presence of their Lord. We shall never see him as he was. In vain our fancy tries to paint it, or our imagination to fashion it. We cannot, must not, see him as he was; nor do we wish, for we have a larger promise: 'We shall shall see him as he *is*.' Come, just look at that a few moments by way of contrast, and then I am sure you will prefer to see Christ as he *is*, rather than behold him as he was.

Consider, first of all, that we shall not see him *abased in his incarnation*, but *exalted in his glory*. We are not to see the infant of a span long; we are not to admire the youthful boy; we are not to address the incipient man; we are not to pity the man wiping the hot sweat from his burning brow; we are not to behold him shivering in the midnight air; we are not to behold him subject to pains, and weaknesses, and sorrows, and infirmities like ours. We are not to see the eye wearied by sleep; we are not to behold hands tired in labour; we are not to behold feet bleeding with arduous journeys, too long for their strength. We are not to see him with his soul distressed; we are not to behold him abased and sorrowful. Oh! the sight is better still. We are to see him exalted. We shall see the head, but not with its thorny crown.

> The head that once was crowned with thorns,
> is crown'd with glory now.

We shall see the hand, and the nail-prints too, but not the nail; it has been once drawn out, and forever. We shall see his side, and its pierced wound too, but the blood shall not issue from it. We shall see him not with a peasant's garb around him, but with the empire of the universe upon his shoulders. We shall see him, not with a reed in his hand, but grasping a golden sceptre. We shall see him, not as mocked and spit upon and insulted, not bone of our bone, in all our agonies, afflictions, and distresses; but we shall see him exalted; no longer Christ the man of sorrows, the acquaintance of grief, but Christ the Man-God, radiant with splendour, effulgent with light, clothed with rainbows, girded with clouds, wrapped in lightnings, crowned with stars, the sun beneath his feet. Oh! glorious vision! How can we guess what *he is?* What words can tell us? or how can we speak thereof! Yet whate'er he is, with all his splendour unveiled, all his glories unclouded, and himself unclothed – *we shall see him as he is.*

Remember again: we are not to see Christ as he was, the *despised*, the *tempted one.* We shall never see Christ sitting in the wilderness, while the arch-traitor says to him, 'If thou be the Son of God command that these stones be made bread.' We shall not see him standing firmly on the temple's pinnacle, bidding defiance to the evil one who bids him cast himself down from his towering height. We shall not see him erect on the mountain of temptation, with the earth offered to him if he will but crouch at the feet of the demon. Nay; nor shall we see him mocked by Pharisees, tempted by Sadducees, laughed at by Herodians. We shall not behold him with the finger of scorn pointed at him. We shall never see him called a 'drunken man and a wine-bibber'. We shall never see the calumniated, the insulted, the molested, the despised Jesus. He will not be seen as one from whom we shall hide our faces, who 'was despised, and we esteemed him not'. Never shall these eyes see those blessed cheeks dripping with the spittle; never shall these hands touch that blessed hand of his while stained with infamy. We shall not see him despised of men and oppressed; but *we shall see him as he is*.

> No more the bloody spear,
> The cross and nails no more;
> For hell itself shakes at his name,
> And all the heavens adore.

No tempting devil near him; for the dragon is beneath his feet. No insulting men; for lo! the redeemed cast their crowns before his feet. No molesting demons; for angels sound his lofty praise through every golden street; princes bow before him; the kings of the isles bring tribute; all nations pay him homage, while the great God of heaven and earth shining on him, gives him mighty honour. We shall see him, beloved, not abhorred, not despised and rejected, but worshipped, honoured, crowned, exalted, served by flaming spirits and worshipped by cherubim and seraphim. '*We shall see him as he is*.'

Mark again. We shall not see the Christ *wrestling with pain*, but Christ *as a conqueror*. We shall never see him tread the winepress alone, but we shall see him when we shall cry, 'Who is this that cometh from Edom, with dyed garments from Bozrah? this that is glorious in his apparel, travelling in the greatness of his strength?' We shall never see him as when he stood foot to foot with his enemy: but we shall see him when his enemy is beneath his feet. We shall never see him as the bloody sweat streams from his whole body; but we shall see him as he hath put all things under him, and hath conquered hell itself. We shall never see him as the wrestler; but we shall see him grasp the prize. We shall never see him sealing the rampart; but we shall see him wave the sword of victory on the top thereof. We shall not see him fight; but we shall see him return from the fight victorious, and shall cry, 'Crown him, Crown him! Crowns become the victor's brow.' '*We shall see him as he is.*'

Yet again. We shall never see our Saviour under his Father's *displeasure*; but we shall see him *honoured by his Father's smile*. The darkest hour of Christ's life was when his Father forsook him – that gloomy hour when his Father's remorseless hand held the cup to his Son's own lips, and bitter though it was said to him, 'Drink, my Son – ay, drink'; and when the quivering Saviour, for a moment, having man within him – strong in its agonies for the moment – said, 'My Father, if it be possible, let this cup pass from me.' Oh! it was a dark moment when the Father's ears were deaf to his Son's petitions, when the Father's eyes were closed upon his Son's agonies. 'My Father,' said the Son, 'Canst thou not remove the cup? Is there no way else for thy severe justice? Is there no other medium for man's salvation?' There is none! Ah! it was a terrible moment when he tasted the wormwood and the gall; and surely darker still was that sad midday–midnight, when the sun hid his face in darkness, while Jesus cried, 'My God, my God, why hast thou forsaken me?'

Believer, thou wilt never see that sick face; thou wilt never see that wan, wan forehead; thou wilt never see that poor scarred brow; thou wilt never see those tearful eyes; thou wilt never see that pale emaciated body; thou wilt never see that weary, weary heart! Thou wilt never see that exceedingly sorrowful spirit; for the Father never turns his face away now. But what wilt thou see? Thou wilt see thy Lord lit up with his Father's light as well as with his own; thou wilt see him caressed by his beloved Parent; thou wilt see him sitting at his Father's right hand, glorified and exalted for ever. *We shall see him as he is.*

Perhaps I have not shown clearly enough the difference between the two visions – the sight of what he was and what he is. Allow me then, a moment more, and I will try to make it clearer still. When we see Christ as he was, how *astonished* we are; one of the first feelings we should have, if we could have gone to the Mount of Olives and seen our Saviour sweating there, would have been astonishment. When we were told that it was the Son of God in agonies, we should have lifted up our hands, and there would have been no speech in us at the thought. But then, beloved, here is the difference. The believer will be as much astonished when he sees Jesus' glories as he sits on his throne, as he would have been to have seen him in his earthly sufferings. The one would have been astonishment, and horror would have succeeded it; but when we see Jesus as he is, it will be *astonishment without horror.* We shall not for one moment feel terrified at the sight, but rather

Our joys shall run eternal rounds,
Beyond the limits of the skies.
And earth's remotest bounds.

If we could see Jesus as he was, we should see him with *great awe.* If we had seen him walking on the water, what awe should we have felt; if we had seen him raising the dead, we should have thought him a most majestic Being. So we shall feel awe when we see Christ on his throne; but the first kind of awe is awe compounded with fear, for when they saw Jesus walking on the water they cried out and were afraid; but when we shall see Christ as he is, we shall say, 'Majestic sweetness sits enthroned upon his awful brow.' There will be no fear with the awe – but it will be *awe without fear.* We shall not bow before him with trembling, but it will be with joy; we shall not shake at his presence, but rejoice with joy unspeakable.

Furthermore, if we had seen Christ as he was, we should have had great *love* for him; but that love would have been compounded with *pity.* We should stand over him, and say,

Alas! and did my Saviour bleed,
And did my Sovereign die?
Would he devote that sacred head
For such a worm as I?

We shall love him quite as much when we see him in heaven, and more too, but it will be *love without pity;* we shall not say 'Alas!' but we shall shout

All-hail, the power of Jesu's name;
Let angels prostrate fall:
Bring forth the royal diadem,
And crown him Lord of all.

Once again. If we had seen Jesus Christ as he was here below, there would have been *joy* to think that he had come *to save us*; but we should have had *sorrow* mingled with it to think that we *needed saving*. Our sins would make us grieve that he should die; and 'alas!' would burst from us even with a song of joy. But when we see him there, it will be *joy without sorrow;* sin and sorrow itself will have gone; ours will be a pure, unmingled, unadulterated joy.

Yet more. If we had seen our Saviour as he was, it would have been a *triumph* to see how he conquered, but still there would have been *suspense* about it. We should have feared lest he might not overcome. But when we see him up there, it will be *triumph without suspense*. Sheathe the sword; the battle's won. 'Tis over now. ' 'Tis finished' has been said. The grave has been past; the gates have been opened; and now, henceforth, and for ever, he sitteth down at his Father's right hand, from whence also he shall come to judge the quick and the dead.

Here, then, is the difference. 'We shall see him as he is.' We shall feel astonishment without horror, awe without fear, love without pity, joy without sorrow, triumph without suspense. That is the glorious position, Poor words, why fail ye; Poor lips, why speak ye not much better? If ye could, ye would; for these are glorious things ye speak of. 'We shall see him as he is.'

Now secondly, we have *personal identity*. Perhaps while I have been speaking, some have said, 'Ah! but I want to see *the* Saviour, the Saviour of Calvary, the Saviour of Judaea, the very one that died for me. I do not so much pant to see the glorious Saviour you have spoken of; I want to see that very Saviour who did the works of love, the suffering Saviour; for him I love.' Beloved, you shall see him. It is the same one. There is personal identity. 'We shall see him.' 'Our eyes shall see him and not another.' 'We shall see *him* as he is.' It is a charming thought that we shall see the very, very Christ; and the poet sung well, who said

> Oh! how the thought that I shall know
> The man that suffered here below,
> To manifest his favour,
> For me, and those whom most I love,
> Or here, or with himself above,
> Does my delighted passion move,
> At that sweet word 'for ever'.
> For ever to behold him shine,
> For evermore to call him mine,
> And see him still before me.
> For ever on his face to gaze,
> And meet his full assembled rays,
> While all the Father he displays,
> To all the saints forever.

That is what we want – to see the same Saviour. Ay, it will be the same Lord we shall see in heaven. Our eyes shall see *him* and not another. We shall be sure it is he; for when we enter heaven we shall know him by his *manhood and Godhead*. We shall find him a man, even as much as he was on earth. We shall find him man and God too, and we shall be quite sure there never was another Man-God; we never read or dreamed of another. Don't suppose that when you get to heaven you will have to ask, 'Where is the man Christ Jesus?' *You* will see him straight before you on his throne, a man like yourselves.

> 'Bright like a man the Saviour sits;
> The God, how bright he shines.'

But then you will know Christ by his *wounds*. Have you never heard of mothers having recognized their children years after they were lost by the marks and wounds upon their bodies? Ah! beloved, if we ever see our Saviour, we shall know him by his wounds. 'But', you say, 'They are all gone.' Oh no; for he

> Looks like a Lamb that once was slain,
> And wears his priesthood still.

The hands are still pierced, though the nails are not there; the feet have still the openings through them; and the side is still gaping wide; and we shall know him by his wounds. We have heard of some who on the battlefield have been seeking for the dead; they have turned their faces up and looked at them, but knew them not. But the tender wife has come, and there was some deep wound, some sabre cut that her husband had received upon his breast, and she said, 'It is he, I know him by that wound.' So in heaven we shall in a moment detect our Saviour by his wounds, and shall say, 'It is he; it is he – he who once said, "They have pierced my hands and my feet."'

But then, beloved, Christ and we are not strangers; for we have often seen him in this glass of the Word. When by the Holy Spirit our poor eyes have been anointed with eye-salve, we have sometimes caught a sufficient glimpse of Christ to know him by it. We have never seen him except reflectedly. When we have looked on the Bible, he has been above us and looked down upon it; and we have looked there as into a looking glass, and have seen him 'as in a glass darkly'. But we have seen enough of him to know him. And oh, methinks when I see him, I shall say, 'That is the bridegroom I read of in Solomon's Song; I am sure it is the same Lord that David used to sing of. I know that is Jesus, for he looks even now like that Jesus who said to the poor woman, "Neither do I condemn thee," – like that blessed Jesus who said "*Talitha Cumi*," – "Maid, I say unto thee, arise."' We shall know him, because he will be so much like the Bible Jesus, that we shall recognize him at once.

Yet more, we have known him better than by Scripture sometimes – by close and intimate *fellowship* with him. Why, we meet Jesus in the dark sometimes; but we have sweet conversation with him, and he puts his lips against our ear, and our lip goes so close to his ear, when we hold converse with him. Oh! we shall know him well enough when we see him. You may trust the believer for knowing his Master when he finds him. We shall not need to have Jesus Christ introduced to us when we go to heaven; for if he were off his throne and sitting down with all the rest of the blessed spirits, we should go up to him directly, and say, 'Jesus, I know thee.' The devil knew him, for he said, 'Jesus I know'; and I am sure God's people ought to know him. 'Jesus, I know thee,' we shall say at once, as we go up to him. 'How dost thou know me?' saith Jesus. 'Why sweet Jesus, we are no strangers, thou hast manifested thyself to me as thou dost not unto the world; thou hast given me sometimes such tokens of thy gracious affection; dost thou think I have forgotten thee? Why, I have seen thy hands and thy feet sometimes by faith, and I have put my hand into thy side, like Thomas, of old; and thinkest thou that I am a stranger to thee? No, blessed Jesus; if thou wert to put thine hand before thine eyes, and hide thy countenance I should know thee then. Wert thou blindfolded once more, mine eyes would tell thee, for I have known thee too long to doubt thy personality.' Believer, take this thought with thee: 'we shall see *him*,' despite all the changes in his position. It will be the same person. We shall see the same hands that were pierced, the same feet that were weary, the same lips that preached, the same eyes that wept, the same heart that heaved with agony; positively the same, except as to his condition. 'We shall see *him*.' Write the word HIM as large as you like. 'We shall see *him* as he is.'

This brings us to the third point – *the positive nature of the vision* – 'We *shall see* him as he is.' This is not the land of sight; it is too dark a country to see *him*, and our eyes are not good enough. We walk here by faith, and not by sight. It is pleasant to believe his grace, but we had rather see it. Well, 'We *shall see* him.' But perhaps you think, when it says, 'We shall see him,' that it means we shall know more about him; we shall think more of him; we shall get better views of him by faith. Oh, no, it does not at all. It means what it says – positive sight. Just as plainly as I can see my brother there, just as plainly as I can see any one of you, shall I see Christ – with these very eyes too. With these very eyes that look on you shall I look on the Saviour. It is not a fancy that we shall see him. Do not begin cutting these words to pieces. Do you see that gas lamp? You will see the Saviour in the same fashion – naturally, positively, really, actually! You will not see him dreamily, you will not see him in the poetical sense of the word – see, you will not see him in the metaphorical meaning of the word; but positively, you shall 'see him as he is'.

'See him', mark that. Not think about him, and dream about him; but we shall positively 'see him as he is'. How different that sight of him will be from that which we have here. For here we see him *by reflection*. Now, I have told you before, we see Christ 'through a glass darkly'; then we shall see him face to face. Good Doctor John Owen, in one of his books, explains this passage, 'Here we see through a glass darkly'; and he says that means, 'Here we look through a telescope, and we see Christ only darkly through it.' But the good man had forgotten that telescopes were not invented till hundreds of years after Paul wrote; so that Paul could not have intended telescopes. Others have tried to give other meanings to the word. The fact is, glass was never used to see through at that time. They used glass to see *by*, but not to see *through*. The only glass they had for seeing was a glass mirror. They had some glass which was no brighter than our black common bottleglass. 'Here we see through a glass darkly.' That means, by means of a mirror. As I have told you, Jesus is represented in the Bible; there is his portrait; we look on the Bible, and we see it. We see him 'through a glass darkly'. Just as sometimes, when you are looking in your looking glass, you see somebody going along in the street. You do not see the person; you only see him reflected. Now, we see Christ reflected; but then we shall not see him in the looking-glass; we shall positively see his person. Not the reflected Christ, not Christ in the sanctuary, not the mere Christ shining out of the Bible, not Christ reflected from the sacred pulpit; but 'we shall see him as he is'.

Again: *how partially we see Christ here*. The best believer only gets half a glimpse of Christ. While here one Christian sees Christ's glorious head, and he delights much in the hope of his coming; another beholds his wounds, and he always preaches the atonement: another looks into his heart, and he glories most in immutability and the doctrine of election; another only looks at Christ's manhood! and he speaks much concerning the sympathy of Christ with believers; another thinks more of his Godhead, and you will always hear him asserting the divinity of Christ. I do not think there is a believer who has seen the whole of Christ. No. We preach as much as we can do of the Master; but we cannot paint him wholly. Some of the best paintings, you know, only just give the head and shoulders; they do not give the full-length portrait. There is no believer, there is no choice divine, that could paint a full-length portrait of Christ. There are some of you who could not paint much more than his little finger; and mark, if we can paint the little finger of Jesus well, it will be worth a lifetime to be able to do that. Those who paint best cannot paint even his face fully. Ah! he is so glorious and wondrous, that we cannot fully portray him. We have not seen him more than partially. Come, beloved; how much dost thou know of Christ? Thou wilt say, 'Ah! I know some little of him; I could join with the spouse, when she declares that he is altogether lovely; but I have not surveyed him from head to foot, and on his wondrous glories I cannot fully dwell.' Here we see Christ partially; there we shall see Christ entirely, when 'we shall see him as he is.'

Here, too, *how dimly we see Christ!* It is through many shadows that we now behold our Master. Dim enough is the vision here; but there 'we shall see him as he is.' Have you never stood upon the hill-tops, when the mist has played on the valley? You have looked down to see the city and the streamlet below; you could just ken yonder steeple, and mark that pinnacle; you could see that dome in the distance; but they were all so swathed in the mist that you could scarcely discern them. Suddenly the wind has blown away the mist from under you, and you have seen the fair, fair valley. Ah! It is so when the believer enters heaven.

Here he stands and looks upon Christ veiled in a mist –
upon a Jesus who is shrouded; but when he gets up there,
on Pisgah's brow, higher still, with his Jesus, then he shall
not see him dimly, but he shall see him brightly. We shall
see Jesus then 'without a veil between' – not dimly, but face
to face.

Here, too, *how distantly we see Christ!* Almost as far off as
the farthest star! We see him, but not nigh; we behold him,
but not near to us; we catch some glimpse of him; but oh!
what lengths and distances lie between! What hills of guilt
– a heavy load! But then we shall see him closely; we shall
see him face to face; as a man talketh with his friend, even
so shall we then talk with Jesus. Now we are distant from
him; then we shall be near to him. Away in the highlands,
where Jesus dwells, there shall our hearts be too, when
heart and body shall be 'present with the Lord'.

And oh! *how transitory is our view of Jesus!* It is only a little
while we get a glimpse of Christ, and then he seems to
depart from us. Our chariots have sometimes been like
Amminadib's; but in a little while the wheels are all gone,
and we have lost the blessed Lord. Have you not some
hours in your life felt so to be in the presence of Christ,
that you scarcely knew where you were? Talk of Elijah's
chariots and horses of fire; you were on fire yourself; you
could have made yourself into a horse and chariot of fire,
and gone to heaven easily enough. But then, all of a sudden,
did you never feel as if a lump of ice had fallen on your
heart, and put the fire out, and you have cried, 'Where is
my beloved gone; Why hath he hidden his face? Oh; how
dark! how dim!' But, Christians, there will be no hidings
of faces in heaven! Blessed Lord Jesus! there will be no
coverings of thine eyes in glory. Is not thine heart a sea

of love, where all my passions roll? And there is no ebb-tide of thy sea, sweet Jesus, there. Art thou not everything? There will be no losing thee there – no putting thy hand before thine eyes up there; but without a single alteration, without change or diminution, our unwearied, unclouded eyes, shall throughout eternity perpetually behold thee. 'We shall see him as he is!' Blest sight! Oh! that it were come!

Then, do you know, there will be another difference. When 'we shall see him as he is', how much better that sight will be than what we have here! When we see Christ here, we see him to our profit; when we see him there, we shall see him *to our perfection*. I bear my Master witness, I never saw him yet, without being profited by him. There are many men in this world whom we see very often, and get very little good by, and the less we see of them the better; but of our Jesus we can say, we never come near him without receiving good by him. I never touched his garments yet, without feeling that my fingers did smell of myrrh, and aloes, and cassia out of the ivory palaces. I never did come near his lips, but what his very breath shed perfume on me. I was never near my Master yet, but what he slew some sin for me. I never have approached him, but his blessed eyes burned a lust out of my heart for me. I have never come near to hear him speak, but I felt I was melting when the Beloved spoke; being conformed into his image.

But, then beloved, it will not be to improve us, it will be to perfect us, when we see him there. 'We shall be like him; for we shall see him as he is.' Oh! that first sweet look on Christ, when we shall have left the body! I am clothed in rags: he looks upon me, and I am clothed in robes of light. I am black; he looks upon me, and I forget the tents of

Kedar, and become white as the curtains of Solomon. I am defiled; sin has looked upon me, and there is filth upon my garments: lo, I am whiter than the driven snow, for he hath looked upon me. I have evil wishes and evil thoughts, but they have fled like the demon before his face, when he said, 'Get thee hence, Satan; I command thee to come out of the man.' 'We shall be like him; for we shall see him as he is.'

I know, beloved, the Saviour seems to you like a great ship, and I like some small boat, trying to pull the ship out of the harbour. It is how I feel myself. I have the oars, I am trying to pull; but it is such a glorious big ship, that I cannot pull it out. There are some subjects the rudder of which I can take hold of and guide anywhere; they will come out of any harbour, let the passage be ever so narrow; but this is a noble ship – so big that we can hardly get it out to sea. It needs the Holy Ghost to blow the sails for you, and your whole souls to dwell upon it and desire to think of this wondrous sight; and then I hope you will go away dissatisfied with the preacher, because you will feel that the subject had altogether mastered him and you also.

Lastly, here are *The Actual Persons*: '*We* shall see him as he is.' Come, now, beloved! I do not like dividing you; it seems hard work that you and I should be split asunder, when I am sure we love each other with all our hearts. Ten thousand deeds of kindness received from you, ten thousand acts of heartfelt love and sympathy, knit my heart to my people. But oh! beloved, is it not obvious, that when we say, '*we* shall see him,' that word 'we' does not signify all of us – does not include everybody here! '*We* shall see him as he is!' Come, let us divide that 'we' into 'I's'. How many 'I's' are there here, that will 'see him as he is'?

Brother, with snow upon thy head, wilt thou 'see him as he is'? Thou hast had many years of fighting, and trying, and trouble: if thou ever dost 'see him as he is', that will pay for all. 'Yes,' sayest thou, 'I know in whom I have believed.' Well, brother, thine old dim eyes will need no spectacles soon. To 'see him as he is', will give thee back thy youth's bright beaming eye, with all its lustre and its fire. But are thy grey hairs full of sin? And doth lust tarry in thy old cold blood? Ah! thou shalt see him, but not nigh; thou shalt be driven from his presence. Would God this arm were strong enough to drag thee to a Saviour; but it is not. I leave thee in his hands. God save thee!

And thou, dear brother, and thou, dear sister, who hast come to middle age, struggling with the toils of life, mixed up with all its battles, enduring its ills, thou art asking, it may be, shalt thou see him! The text says, '*We* shall'; and can you and I put our hands on our hearts and know our union with Jesus? If so, '*We* shall see him as he is.' Brother! fight on! Up at the devil! Strike hard at him! Fear not! that sight of Christ will pay thee. Soldier of the cross, whet thy sword again, and let it cut deep. Labourer! toil again; delve deeper; lift the axe higher, with a brawnier and stouter arm; for the sight of thy Master at last will please thee well. Up, warrior! Up the rampart, for victory sits smiling on the top, and thou shalt meet thy Captain there! When thy sword is reeking with the blood of thy sins, it will be a glory indeed to meet thy master, when thou art clothed with triumph, and then to 'see him as he is'.

Young man, my brother in age, the text says, '*We* shall see him as he is.' Does 'we' mean that young man there in the aisle? Does it mean you, my brother, up there? Shall *we* 'see him as he is'? We are not ashamed to call each other brethren in this house of prayer. Young man, you have got a mother and her soul doats[2] upon you. Could your mother come to you this morning, she might take hold of your arm, and say to you, 'John, we shall "see him as he is"; it is not I, John, that shall see him for myself alone, but you and I shall see him together, "*we* shall see him as he is."' Oh! bitter, bitter thought that just now crossed my soul! O heavens! if we ever should be sundered from those we love so dearly when the last day of account shall come! Oh! if we should not see him as he is!

Methinks to a son's soul there can be nought more harrowing than the thought, that it possibly may happen that some of his mother's children shall see God, and he shall not. I had a letter just now from a person who thanks God that he read the Sermon, 'Many shall come from the east and from the west'; and he hopes it has brought him to God. He says, 'I am one out of a large family, and all of them love God except myself; I don't know that I should have thought of it, but I took up this sermon of yours, and it has brought me to a Saviour.' Oh! beloved, think of bringing the last out of nine to a Saviour! Have not I made a mother's heart leap for joy? But oh! if that young man had been lost out of the nine, and had seen his eight brothers and sisters in heaven, while he himself was cast out, methinks he would have had nine hells – he would be nine times more miserable in hell, as he saw each of them, and his mother and his father, too, accepted, and himself cast out. It would not have been 'we' there with the whole family.

What a pleasant thought it is, that we can assemble today, some of us, and can put our hands round those we love, and

---

2.   a variant of 'dotes'

stand, an unbroken family – father, mother, sister, brother, and all else who are dear, and can say by humble faith, '*We* shall see him as he is' – all of us, not one left out! Oh; my friends, we feel like a family at Park Street. I do feel myself, when I am away from you, that there is nothing like this place, that there is nothing on earth which can recompense the pain of absence from this hallowed spot. Somehow or other, we feel knit together by such ties of love! Last Sabbath I went into a place where the minister gave us the vilest stuff that ever was brewed. I am sure I wished I was back here, that I might preach a little godliness, or else hear it. Poor Wesleyan thing! He preached works from beginning to end, from that very beautiful text – 'They that sow in tears shall reap in joy!', telling us that whatever we sowed, that we should reap, without ever mentioning salvation for sinners, and pardon required even by saints. It was something like this: 'Be good men and women, and you shall have heaven for it. Whatsoever you sow you are sure to reap; and if you are very good people, and do the best you can, you will all go to heaven, but if you are very bad and wicked, then you will have to go to hell; I am sorry to tell you so, but whatever you sow that shall you reap.' Not a morsel about Jesus Christ, from beginning to end; not a scrap. 'Well,' I thought, 'they say I'm rather hard upon these Arminian fellows; but if I do not drive my old sword into them worse than ever, now I have heard them myself again, then I am not a living man!' I thought they might have altered a little, and not preach works so much; but I am sure there never was a sermon more full of salvation by works preached by the Pope himself, than that was. They do believe in salvation by works, whatever they may say, and however they may deny it when you come to close quarters with them; for they are so everlastingly telling you to be good, and upright, and godly, and never directing you first to look to the bleeding wounds of a dying Saviour; never telling you about God's free grace, which has brought you out of enormous sins; but always talking about that goodness, goodness, goodness, which never will be found in the creature. Well, beloved, somehow or other, wherever we go, we seem that we must come back here.

> Here our best friends, our kindred dwell;
> Here God our Saviour reigns.

And the thought of losing one of you grieves me almost as much as the thought of losing any of my relatives. How often have we looked at one another with pleasure! How often have we met together, to sing the same old songs to the same old tunes! How often have we prayed together; And how dearly we all of us love the sound of the word 'Grace, grace, grace!' And yet there are some of you that I know in my heart, and you know yourselves, will not see him, unless you have a change – unless you have a new heart and a right spirit. Well, would you like to meet your pastor at the day of judgment, and feel that you must be parted from him because his warnings were unheeded and his invitation cast to the wind. Thinkest thou, young man, that thou wouldst like to meet me at the day of judgment, there to remember what thou hast heard, and what thou hast disregarded? And thinkest thou, that thou wouldst like to stand before thy God, and to remember how the way of salvation was preached to thee – 'Believe on the Lord Jesus Christ, and be baptized, and thou shalt be saved' – and that thou didst disregard the message? That were sad indeed. But we leave the thought with you, and lest you should think that if you are not worthy you will not see him – if you are not good you will not see him – if you do not do such-and-such good things you will not see him – let me just tell you, whosoever, though he be the greatest sinner under heaven – whosoever, though his life be the most filthy and the most corrupt – whosoever he is, though he has up till now been the most abandoned and profligate – whosoever believeth in the Lord Jesus Christ shall have everlasting life; for God will blot out his sins, will give him righteousness through Jesus, accept him in the beloved, save him by his mercy, keep him by his grace, and at last present him spotless and faultless before his presence with exceeding great joy.

My dear friends, it is a sweet thought to close with now; that with a very large part of you I can say, '*We* shall see him as he is.' For you know when we sit down at the Lord's Table, we occupy the whole ground floor of this chapel, and I believe that half of us are people of God here, for I know that many members cannot get to the Lord's Table in the evening. Brethren, we have one heart, one soul – 'one Lord, one faith, one baptism'. We may be sundered here below a little while; some may die before us, as our dear brother Mitchell has died; some may cross the stream before the time comes for us; but we shall meet again on the other side of the river. 'We shall see him as he is.'

7

The Heavenly Singers and their Song[1]

And when he had taken the book, the four beasts and four and twenty elders fell down before the Lamb, having every one of them harps, and golden vials full of odours, which are the prayers of saints. And they sung a new song, saying, Thou art worthy to take the book, and to open the seals thereof: for thou wast slain, and hast redeemed us to God by thy blood out of every kindred, and tongue, and people, and nation; and hast made us unto our God kings and priests: and we shall reign on the earth.
Revelation 5:8-10

This morning we had a picture of our Lord Jesus Christ appearing in heaven in his sacrificial character, being adored in that character, looking like a Lamb that had been slain, and being worshipped under that aspect in the very centre of heaven. I tried, as far as ever I could, to insist upon it that we must never hide the atoning sacrifice, that Christ, as the Lamb of God which

---

1. Preached at the Metropolitan Tabernacle, Newington, on Lord's Day evening, 14 July 1889.

taketh away the sin of the world, is always to be brought to the front, to be put foremost in our preaching and in our practice, too. In this verse, we go a step further. This blessed Lamb appears in heaven as the Mediator between God and men. At God's right hand was the book of his eternal purposes. None dared even to look upon it; it was hopeless that any creature should be able to loose the seven seals thereof. But there came forward this glorious Lamb, who had the marks of his slaughter upon him, and he took the book out of the right hand of him that sat upon, the throne. Thus he acted as Mediator, Interpreter, taking the will of God, and translating it to us, letting us know the meaning of that writing of the right hand of God which we could never have deciphered, but which, when Christ looses the seals, is made clear to us.

Jesus Christ, then, is seen as our sacrifice in the capacity of Mediator, and in that capacity he becomes the object of the adoration, first, of the Church, then of all the thousands and ten thousands of angels, and then of every creature that God has made. It would be too large a subject to take in all those hallelujahs; and, therefore, in speaking tonight I select only these three verses to set forth the song of the Church, the adoration of the Church of God, rendered to the bleeding Lamb as the Mediator between God and men. I shall have only two divisions. First, behold the worshippers; and, secondly, hearken to their song.

First, *Behold the worshippers*; for, remember, that we must be like them if we are to be with them. It is a well-known rule that heaven must be in us before we can be in heaven. We must be heavenly if we hope to sit in the heavenly places. We shall not be taken up to join the glorified choir unless we have learned their song, and can join their sacred harmony. Look, then, at the worshippers. You are not yet perfectly like them; but you will be, by and by, if you have already the main points of likeness wrought in you by the grace of God.

The first point about the worshippers is this, they are all full of life. I must confess that I should not like to dogmatize upon the meaning of the four living creatures; but still they do seem to me to be an emblem of the Church in its Godward standing, quickened by the life of God. At any rate, they are living creatures; and the elders themselves are living personages. Yet alas, alas, that it should be needful to say so trite a thing; but the dead cannot praise God! 'The living, the living, he shall praise thee, as I do this day.' Yet how many dead people there are in this great assembly to-night! If one, who had sufficient powers of penetration as to be able to detect the actions of the spiritual life of man, were to go round this crowd, 'Ah! me,' he would say, 'take this one away, take that one away; these are dead souls in the midst of the living in Zion.' I will not dwell upon this very solemn thought; but I wish the conscience of some here to dwell upon it when the service is over; you are dead people in the midst of life; you joined in the song just now, but there was no living praise in your singing. Prayer was offered by my dear brother Hurditch very fervently; but there was no living prayer in you. Do you know that it is so? If so, then take your right place; and God grant you enough life to know the absence of life, lest he should say of you, 'Bury my dead out of my sight,' and you should be taken away to the house appointed to the dead, since you cannot be allowed to pollute the gathering of living saints! Those in heaven are all full of life; there is no dead worshipper there, no dull, cold heart that does not respond to the praise by which it is surrounded; they are all full of life.

And further note, that they are all of one mind. Whether they are four and twenty elders, or four living creatures, they all move simultaneously. With perfect unanimity they fall on their faces, or touch their harps, or uplift their golden vials full of sweet odours. I like unanimity in worship here.

You remember the lines —

> At once they sing, at once they pray;
> They hear of heaven, and learn the way.

We used to sing that hymn when we were children; but is there always real unanimity in our assembly? While one is praising, is not another murmuring? While one is earnest, is not another indifferent? While one is believing, is not another an infidel? O God, grant to our assemblies here below the unanimity that comes of the one Spirit working in us the same result, for so we must be in heaven; and if we are not of one mind here below, we are not like the heavenly beings above! When little bickerings come in, when sectarian differences prevent our joining in the common adoration, it is a great pity. God heal his one Church of all her unhappy divisions, and any one church of any latent differences that there may be, that our unity on earth may be an anticipation of the unanimity of heaven!

Note, next, that as the heavenly worshippers are full of life, and full of unity, so they are all full of holy reverence. 'When he had taken the book, the four living creatures and four and twenty elders fell down before the Lamb' – all reverently fell down before the Lamb. And in the fourteenth verse, after their song was over, and after the angels and the whole creation had taken their turn in the celestial music, we read, 'And the four living creatures said, Amen.' It was all that they could say; they were overawed with the majestic presence of God and the Lamb. 'And the four and twenty elders fell down and worshipped him that liveth for ever and ever.' They did not say anything then; they simply fell down and worshipped. It is a grand thing when, at last, we have broken the backs of words with the weight of our feelings, when expressive silence must come in to prove the praises which we cannot utter. It is glorious to be in this reverent state of mind. We are not always so; but they are so in heaven; they are all ready to fall down before the Lord. Do you not think that we often come into our places of worship with a great deal of carelessness? And while the service is going on, are we not thinking of a thousand things? Or if we are attentive, is there enough lowly worship about us? In heaven, they fall down before the Lamb; brothers, sisters, should not we serve God better if we did more of this falling down to worship the Lamb?

Note, next, that while they are all full of reverence, they are all in a praising condition: 'Having every one of them harps.' They did not pass one harp round, and take turns in playing it; nor was there one who had to sit still because he had forgotten his harp; but they had, every one of them, his harp. I am afraid those words do not describe all God's people here tonight. My dear sister, where is your harp? It is gone to be repaired, is it not? My dear brother, where is your harp? You have left it on the willow tree, by the waters of Babylon, so you have not one here. I must confess that sometimes I have not a harp; I could preach a solemn sermon, but I could not so well render the praise. Our dear friend Hurditch seemed to have brought his harp with him tonight; I am glad he praised the Lord so many times for so many mercies. We do not always have our harps with us; but the living creatures and the elders had, all of them, the apparatus for the expression of their holy joy, 'having every one of them harps'. Try to be like the spirits above.

But this is not all; they are all ready for prayer. In heaven there is prayer – we must correct the common mistake about that matter – and there is something to pray for. Although we do not ask the intercession of saints and angels – that were far from Scriptural – still, we believe, that the saints do pray. Are they not crying, 'O Lord, how long?' Why should they not pray, 'Thy kingdom come. Thy will be done in earth, as it is in heaven'? They would understand that prayer better than we do. We know how God's will is not done on earth, but they know how it is done in heaven; and they could pray, 'Thy kingdom come, for thine is the kingdom, and the power, and the glory, for ever, Amen.' How sweetly could their lips move over such words as those! Well, they, all of them, had 'golden vials full of odours'. Are we always furnished and prepared for prayer? This ought to be more easy than always to have a harp; but I am afraid that we have not always our golden vials full of odours; I do not know that they are golden vials at all. I am afraid that ours are of the earth, earthy. But in heaven they have golden vials, pure and precious, and they are full of odours. Sometimes, when you look into your prayer-box, my brother, you have to scrape the bottom to find enough perfume to make even a little incense; but to have our vials full of sweet odours, this is the state of mind in which we should be always. God bring us to that! We shall be getting near heaven, when we can always pray, and certainly near heaven when we can always praise.

> 'Prayer and praise, with sins forgiven,
> Bring to earth the bliss of heaven,'

and make us ready to go up and share that bliss.

Now you see something of what these worshippers were. I do but pause a moment to ask whether we are prepared to go there, whether we are like those who are there. Remember that there is but one place for us besides; if we do not enter heaven, to praise with those perfect spirits, we must be driven from the divine presence to suffer with the condemned. You are not willing to go to hell; will you not be in earnest to go to heaven? You recoil at the idea of 'Depart, ye cursed!' Oh, why not even now accept, 'Come, ye blessed,' while Jesus repeats his gracious invitation, 'Come unto me, all ye that labour, and are heavy laden, and I will give you rest'? I wish that I were able to press this invitation upon you; but I do put it before you. In the name of Jesus, the Lamb of God, that taketh away the sin of the world, I invite you to trust in him, and find your sins forgiven; and so doing, you shall be prepared to meet the Lamb who sits upon the throne, and there for ever to adore his sacrifice, while you enjoy the blessings that flow from it. May we all meet in heaven! It would be a dreadful thing if we could know the destiny of everybody here, and find, among other things, that some here will never see the gate of pearl except from an awful distance, with a great gulf fixed, of which gulf it is said, 'They which would pass from hence to you, cannot; neither can they pass to us, that would come from thence.' May we be on the right side of that gulf! Be on the right side of it tonight, for Jesus' sake!

Now, having thus spoken of the worshippers, I want you to *hearken to their songs*. We must hearken our best in the short time that we have left. 'They sang a new song, saying, Thou art worthy to take the book, and to open the seals thereof:

for thou wast slain, and hast redeemed us to God by thy blood out of every kindred, and tongue, and people, and nation; and hast made us unto our God kings and priests: and we shall reign on the earth.'

It is rather an unusual thing to take a hymn, and treat it *doctrinally* but, for your instruction, I must take away the poetry for a moment, and just deal with the doctrines of this heavenly hymn. The first doctrine is, Christ is put in the front – the deity of Christ, as I hold. They sing, 'Thou art worthy, thou art worthy.' A strong-winged angel sped his way o'er earth and heaven, and down the deep places of the universe, crying with a loud voice, 'Who is worthy to open the book?' but no answer came, for no creature was worthy. Then came One, of whom the Church cries in its song, 'Thou art worthy, thou art worthy.' Yes, beloved, he is worthy of all the praise and honour that we can bring to him. He is worthy to be called equal with God, nay, he is himself God, very God of very God; and no man can sing this song, or ever will sing it, unless he believes Christ to be divine, and accepts him as his Lord and God.

Next, the doctrine of this hymn is that the whole Church delights in the mediation of Christ. Notice, it was when he had taken the book that they said, 'Thou art worthy to take the book.' To have Christ standing between God and man, is the joy of every believing heart. We could never reach up to God; but Christ has come to bridge the distance between us. He places one hand on man and the other upon God; he is the Daysman, who can lay his hand upon both; and the Church greatly rejoices in this. Remember that even the working of providence is not apart from the mediation of Christ. I rejoice in this, that if the thunders be let loose, if plagues and deaths around us fly, the child of God is still under the Mediator's protection, and no harm shall happen to the chosen, for Jesus guards us evermore. All power is given unto him in heaven and in earth, and the Church rejoices in his mediatorship.

But now, notice, in the Church's song, what is her reason for believing that Christ is worthy to be a Mediator. She says, 'Thou art worthy, for thou wast slain.' Ah, beloved, when Christ undertook to be her Mediator, this was the extreme point to which suretyship could carry him, to be slain! And he has gone to the extreme point, and he has paid life for life. 'In the day that thou eatest thereof thou shalt surely die,' was the sentence pronounced upon Adam. The second Adam has died; he has bowed his head to the sentence, he has vindicated the law of God, he has gone to the extreme length of all that his mediatorship could possibly demand of him, and this makes the redeemed lift up the song higher and higher and higher: 'Thou art worthy, for thou wast slain.' Jesus is never more glorious than in his death; his propitiation is the culmination of his glory, after all, as it was the very utmost depth of his shame, Beloved, we rejoice in our Mediator because he died.

Well then, notice, that they sing of the redemption which his death effected, and they do not sing of the redemption of the world. No, not at all: 'Thou wast slain, and hast redeemed us to God by thy blood out of every kindred, and tongue, and people, and nation.' I am not going into a doctrinal discussion tonight. I believe in the infinite value of the atoning sacrifice; I believe that, if God had ordained it to be effectual for the salvation of many more, it was quite sufficient for the divine purpose; but those whom Christ redeemed unto God by his blood are not all mankind. All mankind will not sing this song; all mankind will not be made kings and priests unto God;

and all mankind are not redeemed in the sense in which this song is lifted up to God. I want to know, not so much about general redemption, of which you may believe what you like, but about particular redemption, personal redemption: 'Thou hast redeemed us.' 'Christ loved the Church, and gave himself for it.' 'Thou hast redeemed us to God by thy blood out of every kindred, and tongue, and people, and nation.' My dear hearer, can you join in this song? It is all very well to say, 'Oh, yes! we are all sinners; we are all redeemed.' Stop, stop; are you a sinner? Do you know it? Sinners are very scarce in London. 'Why, there are millions of them!' say you? Yes, yes, yes; nominally, they will say so; but the bona fide sinner, who knows his guilt, is a scarce article.

> A sinner is a sacred thing,
> The Holy Ghost hath made him so.

If there is a real sinner in this house tonight, she will be weeping at my Master's feet, washing those blessed feet with her tears. But as for your sham sinners – they are sinners enough, God knows; but they do not really believe that they are sinners. They have never done anything very wrong, nothing very particular, nothing very important, nothing to break their hearts about. Oh! you – why, you cannot even claim to come in among the sinners, you are a sham even there! But as for redemption, that redemption that redeemed everybody will not do you any good, for it redeemed Judas, it redeemed the myriads that are now in hell. A poor redemption that! The redemption that you want is the redemption that would fetch you right out from your fellow sinners, so that you would be separated unto God, according to that word, 'Come out from among them, and be ye separate, saith the Lord, and touch not the unclean thing, and I will receive you, and will be a Father unto you, and ye shall be my sons and daughters.'

A thing that is redeemed belonged originally to the person who redeems it; and the redeemed of the Lord always were his:'Thine they were,' saith Christ,'and thou gavest them me.' They always were God's. You cannot go and redeem a thing that does not belong to you. You may buy it, but you cannot redeem it. Now, that which belonged originally to God came under a mortgage through sin. We, having sinned, came under the curse of the Law; and though God still held to it that we were his, yet we were under this embargo, sin had a lien upon us. Christ came, and saw his own, and he knew that they were his own. He asked what there was to pay to redeem them, to take them out of pawn. It was his heart's blood, his life, himself, that was required; he paid the price, and redeemed them; and we tonight sing, 'Thou hast redeemed us to God by thy blood out of every kindred, and tongue, and people, and nation.' He has, by redeeming us, separated us to himself, and made us a peculiar people, bought with blood in a special sense out of all the rest of mankind.

I could tell you a great deal about the universal bearings of Christ's redemption, in which I believe, and in the infinite value of that redemption, in which I believe; but I also say that there was, in the design of God, and in the work of Christ, a peculiar form of redemption, which was only for his own people, even as his intercession is, for he says, 'I pray for them, I pray not for the world, but for them which thou hast given me; for they are thine.' Whatever some may think about it, there is a speciality and peculiarity about the redemption of Christ; and this makes the very highest note of the song of heaven, 'Thou hast redeemed us to God by thy blood out of every kindred, and tongue, and people, and nation.' So much about the heavenly hymn doctrinally.

Now about it *experimentally*: 'Thou hast redeemed us to God.' I have said, dear friends, that you cannot sing this song unless you know something of it now. Have you been redeemed? Has the embargo that was on you through sin been taken off you? Do you believe in Jesus Christ? For every man who believeth in Jesus Christ has the evidence of his eternal redemption. Thou hast been bought back with a countless price if thou believest that Jesus is the Christ, and thou art trusting alone in him. That was their experience: 'Thou hast redeemed us.' They felt free; they remembered when they wore their fetters, but they saw them all broken by Christ. Have you been set free? Have you had your fetters broken? Ask the question, and then let us pass on.

This redemption is the ground of their distinction: 'Thou hast redeemed us to God by thy blood.' I heard one, the other day, say of a certain minister, 'Oh! we want another minister. We are tired of this man; he is always talking so much about the blood.' In the last great day, God will be tired of the man who made that speech. God never wearies of the precious blood, nor will his people who know where their salvation lies. They do not, even in heaven, say that it is a dreadful word to mention. 'Oh, but I do not like the word!' says some delicate gentleman. Your lordship will not be bothered with it, for you will not go to heaven. Do not trouble yourself; you shall not go where they sing about the blood. But, mark you, if you ever do go there, you will hear it over and over and over again: 'Thou hast redeemed us to God by thy blood.' How they will ring it out! 'Thou, thou, thou hast redeemed us to God by thy blood.' How they will emphasize that pronoun, 'Thou', and address the praise wholly to Jesus, and sound out that word with the full music of their harps, 'Thou hast redeemed us to God by thy blood.' They are not ashamed of the blood of Jesus up there.

It is this redemption that has made them kings. We cannot realize our kingship to the full here below; though we do in a measure. There is a poor man here, who has but one room to live in; he has no money in his pocket tonight, yet he is a king in the sight of God. There is one here, perhaps, who used to be a drunkard. He could not overcome the evil anyhow; he signed the pledge, wore the blue ribbon, and so on; but still he went back to the drink. By the grace of God he has got his foot upon it now, for he has a new heart and a right spirit. That man is a king; he is a king over his drunken habits. There is one here who used to have a very fierce temper. It was hard to live with him; but Christ has made him a changed man, and now he is a king, ruling over his temper. It is a grand thing to be made a king over yourself. There are some, who have dominion over millions of others, who have never ruled themselves. Poor creatures! Poor creatures! Thank God, if he has given you the mastery of your own nature; that is a glorious conquest; yet this is only the beginning of what is in this song of heaven.

And then they say, 'Thou hast made us priests.' Oh, the poor creatures we have nowadays in the world, who cannot go to Christ except by a priest! They must go to a priest to confess their sins, and go to a priest to get absolution. We have priests not only in the Church of Rome, but elsewhere; we are sorry to see this accursed priestcraft coming in everywhere. Why, some of you people would like your minister to do all your religion for you, would you not? You take a sitting, and leave your religion to your minister. Christ has made every one of his people a priest, and every child of God is as much a priest as

I am; and I am a priest certainly, a priest unto God to offer the spiritual sacrifice of prayer, and praise, and the ministry of the Word. But here is the peculiar joy of all Christians, that God has made them priests. If they do not use their priesthood here, I am afraid that they will never be able to use their priesthood before the throne of God with their fellow priests. This is the melody of the heavenly song, 'Washed in the precious blood, redeemed by that matchless price, we are now made unto our God kings and priests.' Even on earth each saint can sing –

> I would not change my blest estate,
> For all that earth calls good or great;
> And while my faith can keep her hold,
> I envy not the sinner's gold.

Thus have I spoken of the song doctrinally, and experimentally; now let me speak of it *expectantly*. There is something to be expected: 'And we shall reign on the earth.' When John heard that song, the resurrection day had not yet come. These are the spirits before the throne, disembodied; they are expecting the day of the resurrection. When that day will come, who can tell? But when it comes, the dead in Christ shall rise first. Upstarting at the midnight cry, they shall quit their beds of dust and silent clay, and the saints that are alive and remain shall join them. I will not go into the details of that time; but then shall come a period of halcyon bliss. 'The rest of the dead lived not again until the thousand years were finished.' Then shall be a time of the saints' reigning upon the earth. Their life shall be regal; their delights, their joys and their honours shall be equal to those of kings and princes, nay, they shall far exceed them. Do you and I expect to reign upon the earth? It will seem very odd to one who is very poor, obscure, perhaps ignorant, but who knows his Lord, to find that Christ has made him a priest and a king, and that he shall reign even on the earth with him, and then reign for ever with him in glory; but it would be more singular, it would be perfectly monstrous, if we were to assert of some persons, and of some here present, that they would reign on the earth. The man who lives for himself shall never reign on the earth. 'Blessed are the meek: for they shall inherit the earth'; not the men who, in their selfishness, trample down everybody else with iron heel. You shall not reign on the earth; you have lived here simply to hoard money, or to make a name for yourself, or to indulge your passions, or to revenge yourselves upon your fellow men. You reign, Sir? You? God's prison-house is the place for you, not a throne. But when he has made us meek, and humble, and lowly, and reverent, and pure, then we shall become fit to be promoted to this high calling of being priests and kings for Christ unto God in glory, and even here on earth in the day that is coming.

I wish that everybody here would take to searching himself as to whether he is likely to be of that blessed number. Do you with joy accept Christ as your Mediator? Do you see clearly how worthy he is to be the Mediator? Have you been redeemed from among men? Have you been taken away from old associations? Have you broken loose from habits that held you a slave amongst the Egyptians? Have you come into a new society? Has God brought you into a new heaven and a new earth? Has he given you any measure of reigning power over yourself? Do you live as a priest, serving God continually? If you are obliged to keep on saying, 'No, no, no', to all these questions, then what shall I say but 'Come to Christ'? May you come to him tonight! May he tonight begin in you that blessed process that shall make you meet to be partaker of the inheritance of the saints in light, for Jesus' sake! Amen.

Christian Focus Publications

Our mission statement –

STAYING FAITHFUL

In dependence upon God we seek to impact the world through literature faithful to His infallible Word, the Bible. Our aim is to ensure that the Lord Jesus Christ is presented as the only hope to obtain forgiveness of sin, live a useful life and look forward to heaven with Him.

Our books are published in four imprints:

CHRISTIAN
FOCUS

Popular works including biographies, commentaries, basic doctrine and Christian living.

CHRISTIAN
HERITAGE

Books representing some of the best material from the rich heritage of the church.

MENTOR

Books written at a level suitable for Bible College and seminary students, pastors, and other serious readers. The imprint includes commentaries, doctrinal studies, examination of current issues and church history.

CF4•K

Children's books for quality Bible teaching and for all age groups: Sunday school curriculum, puzzle and activity books; personal and family devotional titles, biographies and inspirational stories – because you are never too young to know Jesus!

Christian Focus Publications Ltd,
Geanies House, Fearn, Ross-shire,
IV20 1TW, Scotland, United Kingdom.
www.christianfocus.com